# THE UNITED KINGDOM IN 1980:

## The Hudson Report

# THE UNITED KINGDOM IN 1980:

## The Hudson Report

The Hudson Institute Europe

**Director of Study:**
Edmund Stillman

*By*
James Bellini
William Pfaff
Laurence Schloesing
Edmund Stillman
*With*
Michael Barth

Associated Business Programmes
London

English language edition, except USA and Canada, published by
**Associated Business Programmes Ltd**
**17 Buckingham Gate, London SW1**

Published in the USA and Canada by
**Halsted Press, a division of**
**John Wiley & Sons Inc, New York**

First published 1974
© **Hudson Research Europe, Ltd**

This book has been printed and bound
in Great Britain by
**Burrup, Mathieson & Co. Ltd, London**

**ISBN 0 85227 036 4**

This report is the work of Hudson Europe. The views expressed are those of the authors who have signed it. The Hudson Institutes, which exist in America and in Europe, have no official political or ideological doctrine; they are independent organisations whose sole commitments are to intellectual seriousness and the public interest. They derive their incomes wholly from contract research undertaken for diverse governments and commercial and public organisations.

The present report has been prepared in the public interest and has been financed exclusively by Hudson Europe from its own funds.

*Melius est reprehendant nos grammatici quam non intelligant populi.*
St. Augustine

(It is better that the professors should reproach us than that the people not understand.)

# CONTENTS

# CHAPTER I

## BRITAIN'S CONDITION

"Concerning the state of this kingdom, I could never have imagined to have seen it as it now is, for their people begin to fail, and those that remain, by a continuance of bad successes, and by their heavy burdens, are quite out of heart."

The writer was the British Ambassador to Madrid in the winter of the year 1640, when already, as he put it, "the state of Christendom begins . . . to be unequally balanced." To us there seems a poignancy in his words—for what the English wrote of the Spaniards three centuries ago seems an accurate description of the malaise afflicting Britain today.

That the outlook for Britain is sombre, few will now deny, though the diagnosis of the extent of Britain's plight, and the causes, are still only partial (in both senses of the words: incomplete and biased). Yet hardly a year ago to say that Britain was in a major crisis produced scandalised denial, even derision. Today, to say the same thing risks boredom. A general election has just ended in which all the parties spoke in the rhetoric of crisis. A virtually unanimous agreement now exists that the country is in its worst economic situation since the war—and perhaps since the Great Depression. There is something more: a universal sense in Britain that the economic crisis is linked to a severe deterioration in the country's social and political health. Popular confidence in the competence of government is very low. A tiny minority (seven per cent, according to a poll taken before the election) believes that the political leadership is capable of mastering Britain's problems. As one writer put it just before election day: "We face the internal crisis with the lack of confidence born of long and persistent national failure" (Peter Jenkins, *The Guardian*). Yet a year ago "long and persistent national failure" would have been widely and hotly denied. Something important has changed. There is in Britain, in November 1974, the dawning recognition that the nation is failing—and that, no doubt, is an indispensable first step towards a solution.

The crisis very often is blamed on world events which Britain is powerless to change—the rise in oil prices, the world epidemic of inflation. An acceptance of failure is dangerous when it is linked to a sense of powerlessness, and this is the case in Britain today. The failures are not really understood. Within the country, the positive remedies being put forward are unconvincing. The results of the election in October have widely been interpreted as a popular choice for the "lesser evil" of the alternatives offered and are devoid of any real positive commitment. The men who did express the belief that they could solve the country's problems through drastic changes—the "new" Labour left, the Selsdon men—were rejected. A choice was made by the voters—for Labour, but Labour on a short leash. As far as election results can say anything, the

1

electorate in October was confused as to the real alternatives open to it. That confusion produced a parliamentary balance with no clear line, a balance that had the incidental quality of minimising risk. It was no vote of confidence.

This report, then, is not meant to tell the British that their country is in trouble. They already know that. We are trying to do something else: to examine *why* the country is in trouble—which, for all the discussion and controversy, seems to us very widely misunderstood. Beyond that, we want to make a contribution to the urgently-needed debate on what Britain can do to get out of trouble.

We must, however, say an introductory word about how this book came about. Hudson Europe, an international research group, published a study of the French economic outlook in the spring of 1973. While we were preparing that study we were forced to pay attention to the contrasts, and they were dramatic contrasts, between the economic and social condition of modern France and that of Britain since the Second World War. In our report on France, which was published in French as *L'Envol de la France* (Hachette Littérature), we noted many of these differences and made some comparisons between the two countries.

These comparisons were taken up by the British press, mostly with scepticism or expressed disbelief, but also with interest in why the French performance might be so different. We then decided to make an examination of the British situation. We sought sponsorship in Great Britain for such a study (our report on France had been contracted by the French Government). We were unsuccessful in this effort, although our proposal was listened to with some interest by many in the country and had an effect even then upon an emerging British debate. The figures and formulations of our 1973 proposal made a later appearance in the September 24, 1973, speech by Lord Rothschild, head of the Cabinet "think tank", when he also warned of the dangers posed by long-range trends in the country.

We might have stopped at that point, content at having helped stimulate a British re-examination of the national situation. In 1972 there had been a great deal of exceedingly foolish optimism about the British outlook—as there is again today when North Sea oil is taken as the solution to basic national problems. But we decided to go ahead because we felt that we might also be able to move the discussion ahead to a second stage, where basic remedies are considered.

The authors of the study include one Briton, a Frenchwoman, a Dutchman, and two Americans. The work has been helped by a good many other people, most of them British, and by a technical and administrative staff mostly French. But why should French and Dutch and Americans interest themselves to this extent in what happens to Britain, or presume to intervene in a basically national matter? The answer, surely, is that Britain has been one of the crucial human societies, and to paraphrase one of its great men, its difficulties diminish us all. There are not many countries of which it can be said that they made a difference to humanity—that their contributions of intelligence, institutions, and art, of constitutional government and social order, have been such that without them the world would be a very different place. Britain is such a country. France no doubt is also. The Netherlands and the United States probably will be given a lesser ranking in the ultimate judgement of history, despite the past accomplishments and the humanity of the Netherlands' present society, and despite the United States' constitutional and social innovations. The British contribution to the world has been a primary one. No one can be indifferent to it. And thus Western Europeans and Americans may perhaps be permitted to feel that they have a certain right to speak of the fate of Britain. We would therefore ask that if this study seems a kind of presumption, an uninvited intervention into Britain's affairs, that it might also be acknowledged as an intervention whose severity comes with goodwill and out of respect for what Britain is and was as a country and what it will become in the future.

**The nature of the crisis**
There is something that must be said at the start. The British crisis is basically an economic crisis—whatever else may lie behind it. It is a failure to grow industrially and economically at the same rate at which other neighbouring countries are growing. But is economic growth so important? Anyone who looks about him at landscapes ruined by heavy industry, or heaped with mine slag, or at poisoned rivers, or who considers the nature of much modern factory and bureaucratic work, or who reflects upon the triviality or ugliness of so much that industry produces, is justified in asking that question. If Britain today, and Britain historically, is a serious nation, this has not come about simply because Britain has been a major industrial producer or, by the standards of the world as a whole, because it has been a rich society. It is because Britain has been an innovative society, a place of ideas and of art, a country which has established a standard of justice.

There thus are those in Britain today who would ignore, or who rationalise, the economic retardation of the country because they believe modern industry and the practical values of industrialism are aesthetically and morally objectionable. Or they say that these issues are irrelevant to what is really important in Britain's society and future. We will address some of these arguments in a later chapter. At this point we will make only a short response. Those who object to industry and growth must tell us how people are to be fed and clothed without it. Britain is not a self-sufficient country and its standard of living is in decline. Even if the British people were willing to adopt a radically changed social system and sacrifice many of today's luxuries (and there are no signs that they are), Britain would still find itself faced with how to supply for itself the necessities of life. It must trade simply to have enough food.

One may with good reason take a highly-qualified view of growth, or oppose

3

certain kinds of growth, or point out the costs and social consequences of certain types of growth, but one must also honestly face what growth or retardation means for Britain's population as a whole. No doubt for some it brings disadvantages because a general rise in living standards tends to reduce the comparative privileges of the well-to-do. But it has been one of the chief justifications—and it is a *moral* justification—of modern industrial society that it gives a better life to the *mass* of people.

The British standard of life in international terms is already far lower than most people realise. The levels of personal income, of health and education, of housing and amenity, are already well below the levels of Britain's major neighbours on the continent. The standard of life in Britain today is only marginally better than that of countries which the British people are accustomed to think of as the "poor" states of the Mediterranean and the Balkans. The majority of Spaniards and Greeks will, on present trends, be better off than the average Briton within not many more years. These facts simply are not understood in Britain. We will, in the chapters which follow, present the statistics, gathered from the standard authorities, the OECD, the UN, the World Bank, the British Government's own admirable statistical services, which prove that these things are so.

When the British look at Western Europe today they often explain away its economic prosperity and growth as achieved by sacrificing a humane society. Growth is pictured as a ruthless process devouring not only an historical landscape but making life worse for people in every way but the narrowly economic. The Germans, it is suggested, have been turned into automatons; urban life in Paris or Milan or Rome is said to be a hellish struggle against the automobile and the wrecker's ball, with the air polluted, the arts and theatre deprived. Britain, it is implied, is better off without these changes. Life in Britain, it is said, remains civilised.

But a moment's examination of the facts about pollution, urban problems, and social unrest, shows that these things are not true. Obviously there are big pollution problems in Italy—one consequence of the weakness of the central government. Obviously Paris is not a museum of the *belle époque*. But Britain has exactly the same kinds of problems as Europe—more of some, less of others—but it has them without the compensating advantages of prosperity. Growth for the ordinary citizen means better housing, a new kitchen with new appliances, good and improving schools for his children, a steadily improving health service and pension plan, a foreign holiday. In not one of these matters does life in Britain today compare favourably with the dynamic European countries. We will give the figures showing comparisons between Britain and France, Germany, the Netherlands, and Italy in a later chapter, but here we must simply say that in virtually every one of the tangible indices of quality of life, Britain is worse off than continental Western Europe. Clearly the tangible indices do not measure all that is meant by the phrase "quality of life", but the things they do measure are indispensible components in a "quality of life" for the

4

mass of people in a developed society. In Britain, these comparative facts are not widely known. The popular belief reflects the past—when Britain *was* more prosperous than the continental countries. Today things have changed. The British do not grasp how much they have changed.

It is our view that accelerated economic growth is, for the British today, a necessity. It will not bring unalloyed benefits, even if Britain can achieve it, which is not at all certain. The ultimate implications of industrialism for all of us remain obscure, and some of these implications that we can perceive are disquieting. The materialistic and rationalist revolution which Britain bestowed upon the rest of the world some three hundred years ago has far from run its course, and much inhumanity has already come from it and no doubt more will be forthcoming. But in this report we are discussing the immediate problems of British society today, and in this society an economic and industrial revival is necessary if very grave social and political problems are to be avoided. Without that revival, life in Britain may become very unpleasant indeed.

**Britain's crisis is unique**
If the world as a whole, or the developed world, or all of the countries of Western Europe, faced the same troubles as Great Britain, one could worry a good deal less about Britain. In fact, as we will show in this book, things are not only worse in Britain than elsewhere but the reasons why they are so bad are not the same reasons that make things bad in certain other countries. The situation here is different in basic ways. Thus the possibilities for a solution are not the same that exist elsewhere. Taken as a whole, the British problem today is unique.

And Britain is not a country which can live in isolation. It is not an insulated nation and economy. The old parochialism of Britain, that psychological isolation which existed at the same time that Britain was the world's leading industrial nation, was possible only so long as Britain was rich. The British assumption of superiority then was validated by economic and industrial pre-eminence. Today, a poor Britain might try to console itself by pretending an indifference to the life and standards of Europe and of North America, but this could not be sustained. In too many practical matters—such as imports and currency—Britain would be affected. The influences of modern politics and mass communications are too powerful. Isolation is not possible, and without isolation the comparisons will be borne home to the average Briton. The differences between life in Britain and life in the other advanced countries would become increasingly evident—and increasingly painful to bear.

It was possible until fairly recently for the British to avoid the truth about their comparative situation because of the powerful national sense of isolation and superiority. Even today, in the shock of discovering the crisis, debates over what to do, even radical reappraisals, reveal much the same provincialism.

5

It is not symptomatic of the British condition that none of the major leftist or radical groups, to say nothing of the Labour Party itself, has any serious tie to continental socialism. Labour, as a party and a social class, is undoubtedly the single most hostile group in Britain to any continental link. While it must be said that Europe (membership in the EEC, that is) cannot save Britain from its present troubles (we will comment on Britain's relation to the European community in a later chapter), the hostility of the British people and British élite to the continent demonstrates just how parochial this nation has become. It is as if there were nothing at all to learn from the modern European experience.

This indifference to Europe, and hostility towards the Europeans, has profound historical sources, of course. These are reinforced by the political and religious differences between Anglo-Saxon and continental cultures. In the recent past Britain's prosperity and the stability of its institutions clearly set it off from the troubled affairs of Europe. But Britain today acts as if there are tangible and institutional superiorities still manifest. There are not.

The present reality is that it is Britain that is the unstable and socially divided nation, economically depressed. Today, the continental states, overall, have not only a vastly better economic performance but also superior popular standards of living and amenity—and they enjoy, overall, a rather more impressive political condition. Even Italy, supposedly the other sick man of Europe, suffers mainly from a political ineptitude that, in its effect upon the society as a whole, is rather less important than ineptitude in Britain's leadership. The Italian state, as such, is in important respects irrelevant to what happens in Italian society. The dynamism of Italian society and of the Italian economy, and in many places of the regional and urban governments of Italy, gives better reason for optimism than is possible to feel when considering Britain today. Italy's problems are those of obsolescent institutions in a vitally developing society; the Italian crisis derives from the bursting of old structures under the power of social change and development, and the vigour of the industrial economy. Britain's problems consist of a decline in both governmental competence and economic performance: a universal loss of dynamism. The distinction is a fundamental one.

**The scale of the crisis**
Our argument is that Britain's economic troubles are very serious because they carry within them the germination of social and political crises. The social concord of Britain is generally thought to be strong, and rightly so, but it is not impregnable. Already some questions exist as to the continued national cohesion and social peace of the country as a united kingdom. The class implications of much recent political controversy is not reassuring; old class wounds, never fully healed, have re-opened under the pressures of the country's economic retardation and failures. As the comparisons between living standards in Britain and those prevailing in Europe become more widely understood, the tensions within Britain will worsen not least because those differences in living

6

standards will increasingly find counterparts amongst the regions of Britain itself.

The present-day nationalism of Scotland and Wales may still be minimal; talk of military dictatorship in London may be absurd; yet the anxieties and sense of frustration that inspire them, and also the revolutionary rhetoric that may be heard on the left, must not be underestimated. Too many people are willing to blame "the others" for the country's troubles, or to look outside Britain for both the cause of those troubles and their cure, or to put their whole faith in some *deus ex machina,* such as North Sea oil, to save the nation from the need for basic change.

We hold that Britain's fundamental troubles come from within the society, and from certain economic, social, and institutional forces which are peculiarly British: aspects of British culture and an inheritance of a particular British historical experience. This book, then, is intended to identify and examine certain of the major factors in the present crisis, and to suggest certain things that might be done to resolve the crisis—if the crisis is indeed to be solved. It is a contribution to a debate. We do not bring to that debate any extraordinary revelations, nor do we offer a comprehensive cure. We will attempt to contribute a certain realism about what economics mean to Britain's political and social peace now and in the future, as well as a certain international perspective too often lacking in Britain's own discussions.

The argument we will make in the pages which follow comes down to this:

The crisis is serious. In fundamental respects it is a crisis unique to Britain, with British causes. Thus, only the British can solve it.

It is more than an economic crisis, but if British economic growth and economic competitiveness could be restored the country would be a long way towards resolving its larger problems.

On the other hand, if the economic problems are not solved, there is serious reason to fear an eventual social and political upheaval in the country.

Finally, while solutions to the strictly economic problems are difficult, and require a certain re-ordering of larger priorities in British society, they are not impossible. Economic renewal is a practical and tangible national goal. Things can be done to make it happen. We will propose some things that may help.

7

# CHAPTER II

## BRITAIN'S PERFORMANCE—
## TODAY AND TOMORROW

The British public either fails to recognise or misunderstands the problems facing the economy in spite of the discussions that take place every day. Using standard sources of data, national and international statistical research organisations, it is possible to express Britain's economic problems in the following way:

1. Lowest growth rate of all developed countries.
2. Uncompetitive economy.
3. Deteriorating balance of payments.
4. Declining standard of living.

Accepting that these things are true, the causes and the implications are best understood by making comparisons with the other industrialised countries. As a basis for reference, we will ordinarily make use of the four major Western European countries: France, Italy, Germany, and the Netherlands; two other rapidly growing countries: Japan and Spain; and finally the United States because of its many similarities with Britain. International comparisons are frequently avoided in the debate within Britain, and the argument is made that what chiefly matters is the domestic situation and its evolution. The contention is heard that Britain has reached a stage of maturity which implies low growth and thus that it does not make any difference whether Britain's neighbours grow twice or even three times as rapidly. For reasons which will be made clear below, we believe that this is wrong. In our opinion it is vital that Britain grows as rapidly as its neighbours and competitors.

### Low growth in Britain
Of all the industrialised and developed economies, Britain has always had one of the lowest growth rates. Between 1949 and 1963 Britain's annual growth was at the rate of 2.6 per cent. This compares with 4.6 per cent in France, 7.8 per cent in Germany, and 5.8 per cent in Italy. Over the last 18 years it has averaged 2.8 per cent, less than half the average growth rate of the French, the Italians and the Spaniards, two-thirds that of the Dutch, and four-fifths that of the US. On a ten-year average since 1963, the result is the same. And most recently (1970), there has been no improvement apart from an exceptional year in 1973 when Britain's GNP grew by 5.4 per cent following a reflationary policy of the government. In fact, since 1955, the GNP has grown by more than 4 per cent on only four occasions: in 1959, 1963, 1964 and 1973. Each of those years was ordinarily followed by deterioration in the balance of payments, deflationary measures to compensate for this, and a period of further low growth.

Chart I

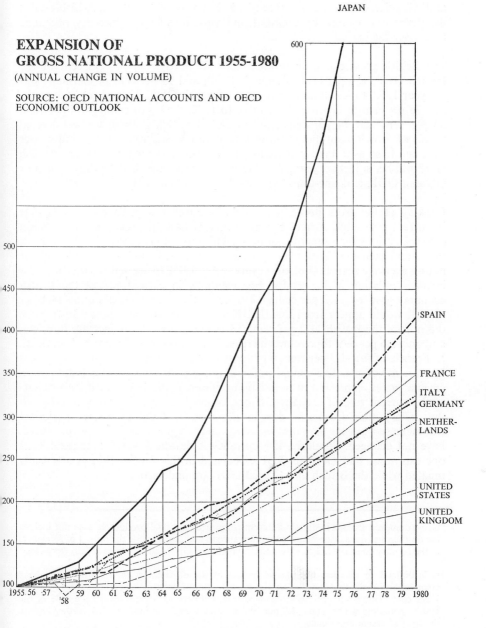

JAPAN

# EXPANSION OF
# GROSS NATIONAL PRODUCT 1955-1980
(ANNUAL CHANGE IN VOLUME)

SOURCE: OECD NATIONAL ACCOUNTS AND OECD
ECONOMIC OUTLOOK

9

This record of low growth has caused the British economy to decline in size by comparison with its neighbours. We will express what has happened in percentages based on US dollars so as to allow for international comparisons, but at 1963 prices and exchange rates. This is a way of calculating which avoids the distortions caused by inflation and variations in the currency exchange rates over the period we consider.

The British gross domestic product* has declined from 112 per cent of the French GDP, 156 per cent of Japan's GDP, and 93 per cent of Germany's in the year 1960, to less than 85 per cent of French GDP, 72 per cent of Japan's, and 76 per cent of Germany's in 1970. In 1972, the ratios came to 74 per cent, 64 per cent and 74 per cent respectively. By 1980, if these well-established trends of growth continue (even at a relatively slower rate—1 per cent slower than before so as to take into account the consequences of the oil crisis,† British GDP will be, in just six years, only some 60 per cent the size of either French or German GDP, and one-third the size of Japan's (Chart II).

Looking at the gross domestic product in another way, expressed this time in current prices and current exchange rates (Chart III), relationships between countries follow the same overall trend. This type of comparison, using current prices and exchange rates, is the one most often made, but in our opinion it is not an accurate reflection of the reality. First, GDP expressed in current prices includes inflation in its results. For example, in current prices, the British economy grew by 11.2 per cent in 1972, and the French economy by 11.5 per cent. It would appear from this that Britain did as well as France. In fact she did not: of the British 11.2 per cent, 7.7 per cent was simply increase in prices, and only 3.5 per cent represented increase in volume (or *real* goods and services). In France, of the 11.5 per cent, 6 per cent was increase in prices and 5.5 per cent increase in volume. The second pitfall in this way of calculating is that GDP at current prices, expressed in national currencies, is then calculated into dollars at the current rate of exchange. If one country revalues its currency (*vis-a-vis* the dollar), then from one day to the next its GDP expressed in dollars will increase—but the standard of living, and the goods and services produced, have not changed. Similarly, if a currency is devalued, GDP decreases. Thus one can argue that German GDP calculated in this way in 1972 is artificially inflated while the British and French GDP are underestimated.

---

*Gross domestic product is slightly different from gross national product. It does not include the output of citizens or companies working abroad and does include the output of foreigners in the country concerned. The variations in volume of GNP and GPD are usually very close.

†It is difficult to measure the precise impact of the oil crisis in each country. We have assumed arbitrarily that it will slow the growth rates of most developed countries by about 1 per cent. This is an optimistic view, assuming no world depression. In the case of the United Kingdom we assume a 1·9 per cent average growth rate up to 1980—rather high in the light of recent experience.

10

# GROSS DOMESTIC PRODUCT AT 1963 PRICES AND EXCHANGE RATES

(IN BILLION U.S. DOLLARS)

SOURCE: OECD NATIONAL ACCOUNTS

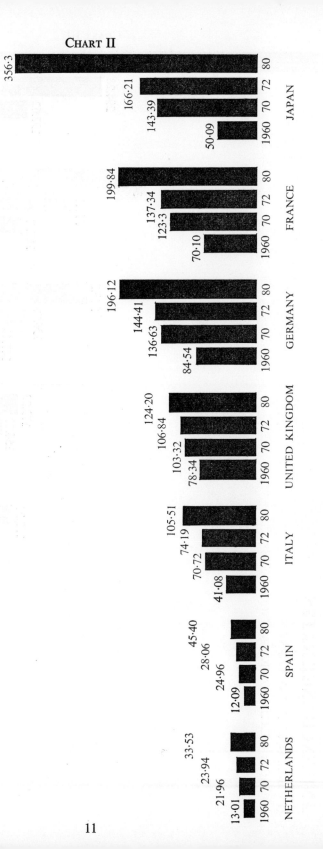

**CHART II**

JAPAN
- 80: 356·3
- 72: 166·21
- 70: 143·39
- 1960: 50·09

FRANCE
- 80: 199·84
- 72: 137·34
- 70: 123·3
- 1960: 70·10

GERMANY
- 80: 196·12
- 72: 144·41
- 70: 136·63
- 1960: 84·54

UNITED KINGDOM
- 80: 124·20
- 72: 106·84
- 70: 103·32
- 1960: 78·34

ITALY
- 80: 105·51
- 72: 74·19
- 70: 70·72
- 1960: 41·08

SPAIN
- 80: 45·40
- 72: 28·06
- 70: 24·96
- 1960: 12·09

NETHERLANDS
- 80: 33·53
- 72: 23·94
- 70: 21·96
- 1960: 13·01

11

# GROSS DOMESTIC PRODUCT AT CURRENT PRICES AND EXCHANGE RATES

(IN BILLION U.S. DOLLARS)
SOURCE: O.E.C.D. NATIONAL ACCOUNTS

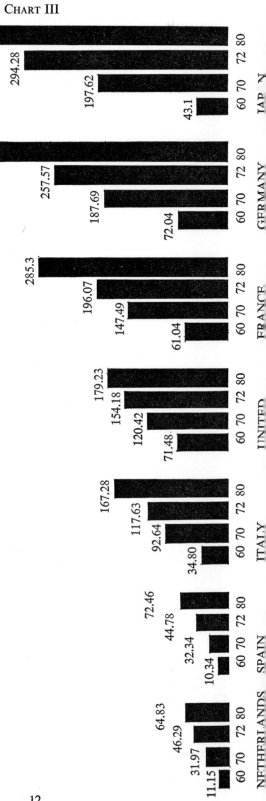

CHART III

**JAPAN**
- 60 70: 43.1
- 60 70: 197.62
- 72 80: 294.28
- 80: 631

**GERMANY**
- 60 70: 72.04
- 60 70: 187.69
- 72 80: 257.57
- 80: 349.8

**FRANCE**
- 60 70: 61.04
- 60 70: 147.49
- 72 80: 196.07
- 80: 285.3

**UNITED**
- 60 70: 71.48
- 60 70: 120.42
- 72 80: 154.18
- 80: 179.23

**ITALY**
- 60 70: 34.80
- 60 70: 92.64
- 72 80: 117.63
- 80: 167.28

**SPAIN**
- 60 70: 10.34
- 60 70: 32.34
- 72 80: 44.78
- 80: 72.46

**NETHERLANDS**
- 60 70: 11.15
- 60 70: 31.97
- 72 80: 46.29
- 80: 64.83

CHART IV AND CHART V

# GROSS NATIONAL PRODUCT PER CAPITA 1971-1980

(IN U.S. DOLLARS)* SOURCE: WORLD BANK ATLAS
*AT A 1965-1971 WEIGHTED AVERAGE EXCHANGE
RATE

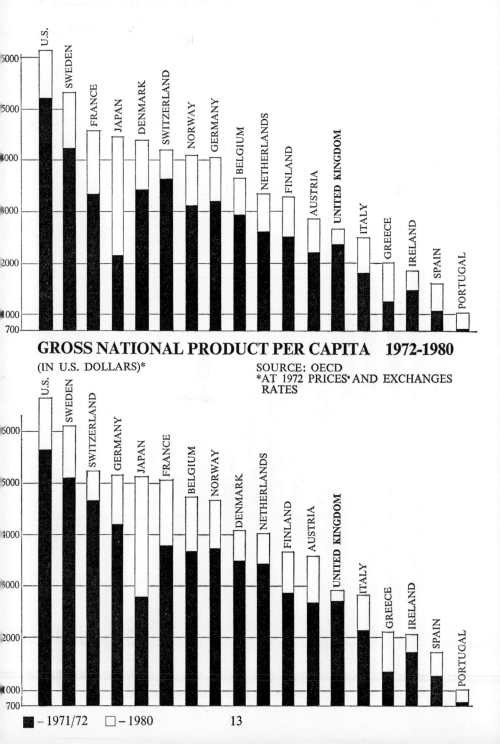

# GROSS NATIONAL PRODUCT PER CAPITA 1972-1980

(IN U.S. DOLLARS)* SOURCE: OECD
*AT 1972 PRICES' AND EXCHANGES
RATES

■ – 1971/72 □ – 1980 13

CHART VI

# GROSS NATIONAL PRODUCT PER CAPITA 1970-1980
## (IN 1970 DM AND PURCHASING POWER PARITIES)
### SOURCE: WORLD BANK ; STATISTICHES BUNDESAMT, WIESBADEN ; O.E.C.D.

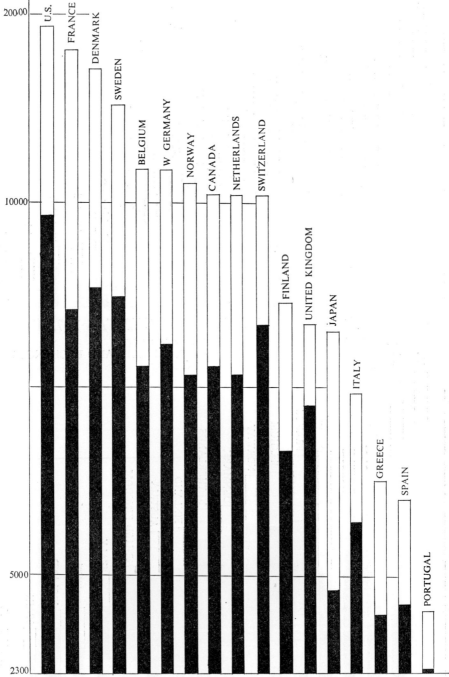

Whichever way it is calculated, the size of the British economy still shows the same trend—a constant decline in relation to its neighbours. In current prices and exchange, Britain was about the same size as the German economy in 1960 but only 60 per cent their size in 1972. A figure of 50 per cent must be projected for 1980. In comparison with France, Britain will drop from 120 per cent of the size of the French economy in 1960 to a projected two-thirds its size in 1980.

**Individual wealth**
Slow growth in Britain has meant that British *per capita* GNP is also dropping to a level that is one of the lowest among the industrialised countries. *Per capita* GDP or GNP is often taken as a rough measure of the wealth of the average inhabitant of a country. It is a rough measure because it is an average and assumes an equal distribution of wealth (a condition that does not exist in any country). It is most inaccurate in the case of the less-developed countries of the Third World where wealth tends to be concentrated in a very small part of the population. However, for countries of similar development it can be a useful tool of comparison.

We will take the figures given by the OECD for 1972. Ranking GDP *per capita* expressed in US dollars at current prices and exchange rates, we find that Britain's *per capita* GDP comes eleventh of eighteen (Chart V). Britain already is behind all of its major European neighbours except Italy. Projecting six years into the future, to 1980, Britain becomes thirteenth, about the same as Italy and followed only by Greece, Ireland, Spain, and Portugal, among the OECD's member states.

Using constant dollars and prices, there is no significant change in the ranking for Britain.*

---

*The main difference concerns the position of France and Germany, presently very close. In current prices and exchange rates, with the devaluation of the French franc and the revaluation of the German currency, French *per capita* GDP is in our opinion undervalued while Germany's is overvalued. This discrepancy in the data is why in Chart IV German GDP becomes higher than the French in 1980, while in constant dollars French GDP in 1980 is far above German GDP (Chart V).

15

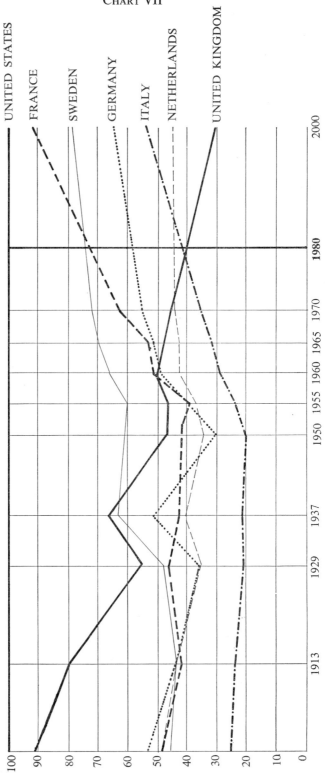

## CHART VII

# HISTORICAL TRENDS IN GROSS NATIONAL PRODUCT
# PER CAPITA    1899-1980

(IN PERCENT OF U.S. GNP PER CAPITA)
SOURCE: COMPUTED FROM WORLD BANK DATA

%

UNITED STATES

FRANCE

SWEDEN

GERMANY

ITALY

NETHERLANDS

UNITED KINGDOM

*AT FACTOR COSTS AND 1969 U.S. DOLLARS
NOTE: THIS GRAPH ONLY SHOWS HISTORICAL TRENDS

100 90 80 70 60 50 40 30 20 10 0

1913 1929 1937 1950 1955 1960 1965 1970 1980 2000

16

Chart VIII

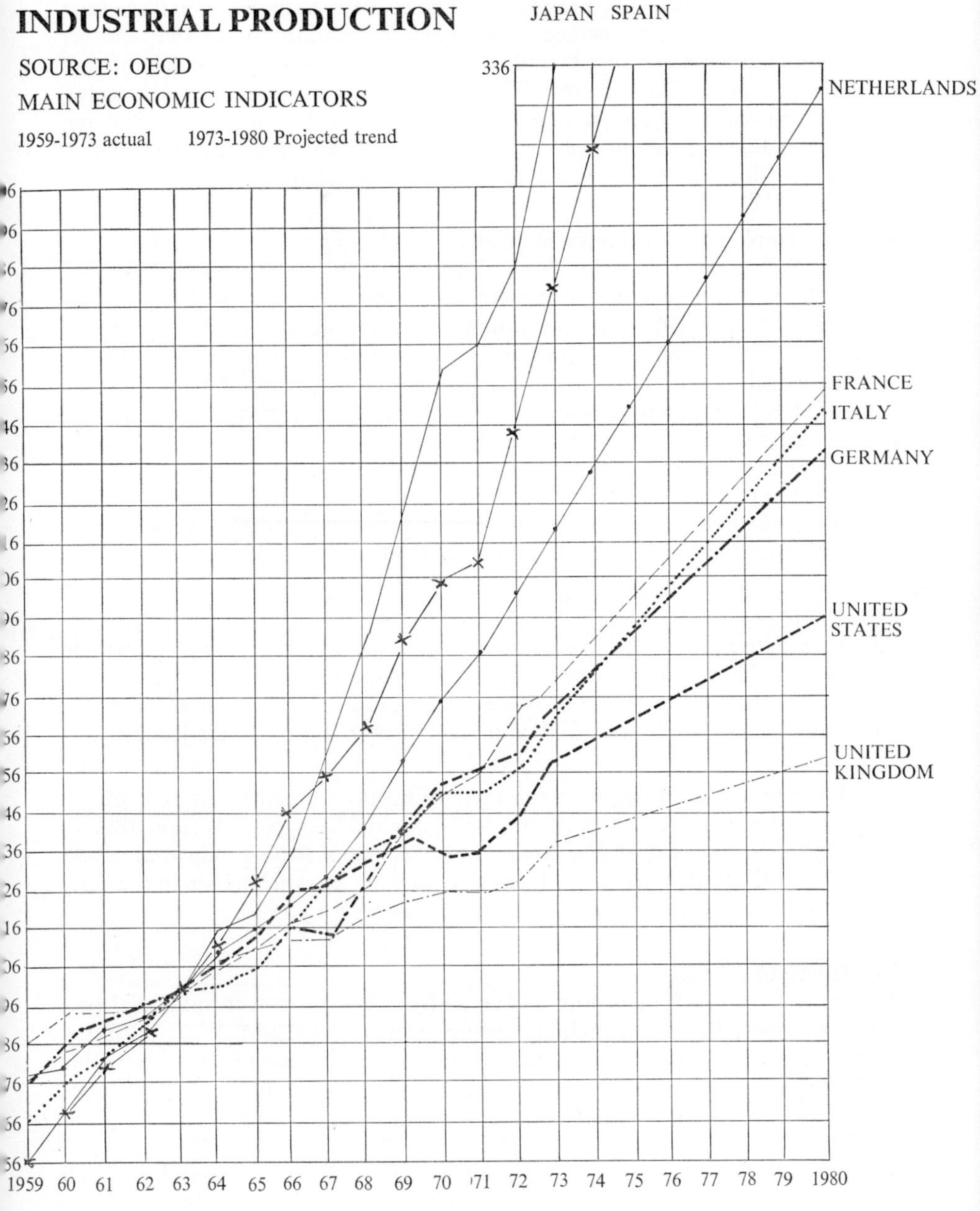

# INDUSTRIAL PRODUCTION

JAPAN  SPAIN

SOURCE: OECD
MAIN ECONOMIC INDICATORS

1959-1973 actual    1973-1980 Projected trend

NETHERLANDS

FRANCE
ITALY

GERMANY

UNITED
STATES

UNITED
KINGDOM

336

1959  60  61  62  63  64  65  66  67  68  69  70  '71  72  73  74  75  76  77  78  79  1980

17

Finally, we can attempt to establish the present and probable future rankings in wealth according to yet a third criterion. This is to employ what is known to economists as purchasing power parities. The concept is simple, even if the term is formidable. Different currencies fluctuate in relationship to one another according to the laws of supply and demand, as well as according to a host of psychological and political factors. These distort comparisons. One can attempt, therefore, to compare gross national product per head by taking into account *the internal value* of the money, i.e., by taking into account what the different currencies will actually buy within their country of origin.

Here we employ the estimates of relative purchasing power prepared by the Federal Statistical Office in West Germany (the Statistiches Bundesamt, Wiesbaden). If we project the growth performance of the British economy between 1960 and 1970 into the future—and we stress that, despite the oil crisis, the *relative* growth performances of the different countries of the developed world remain more or less the same, even if in absolute terms they are somewhat weaker, then we find that Britain which was number eleven in 1970 falls to the rank of thirteenth by 1980 (Chart VI).† In these terms, Britain's wealth per head, which was 64 per cent of the United States level in 1970, will be only 48 per cent in 1980. Compared to France the wealth per head falls from 78 per cent in 1970 to 56 per cent in 1980; while compared to West Germany the respective numbers are 85.5 per cent in 1970 versus 69.6 per cent ten years later.

All these figures, be it said, assume a continuing average annual growth in wealth for Britain—an assumption which, as we shall see below, may itself now be in doubt. In a future world of fierce competition for scarce resources at ever increasing prices Britain may find continued growth itself in some jeopardy.

Chart VII plots the GNP *per capita* of the European countries as percentages of the GNP *per capita* of the United States for different periods from 1899 to 1980. It illustrates the dramatic comparative decline of British industrial wealth since the 1890's with France and Germany catching up with Britain in the early sixties, and Italy in a position to reach Britain's level by 1980.

### The failure to produce
Low growth of GNP in Britain has come from low growth in industrial production, especially in the manufacturing sectors. As Chart VIII illustrates, industrial output in Britain has risen at a rate far below that of any of the other main industrialised countries. In general, industrial output in the developed

---

†Chart VI is a more optimistic alternative assuming continuation of 1960 growth rates until the end of the present decade. It should be noted, nevertheless, that in all three alternative calculations of GNP, the relative position of the UK remains virtually the same.

18

countries tends to rise on an average of 1 per cent faster than GNP. In Britain, over the 1960-70 period, it grew at a rate slightly less than that of GNP. The only sectors in Britain to have experienced significant growth were the chemical industry (including petroleum and coal) and utilities (gas and electricity) —a trend which can be observed in the other countries too. The textiles, food, and clothing sectors, as well as the basic metals sector, traditional low-growth industries, did worst. But the manufacturing sector as a whole did not do much better.

CHART IX

# INVESTMENT AS PERCENTAGE OF G.D.P.

(CURRENT PRICES)

SOURCE: O.E.C.D. NATIONAL ACCOUNTS

1955

1965

1972

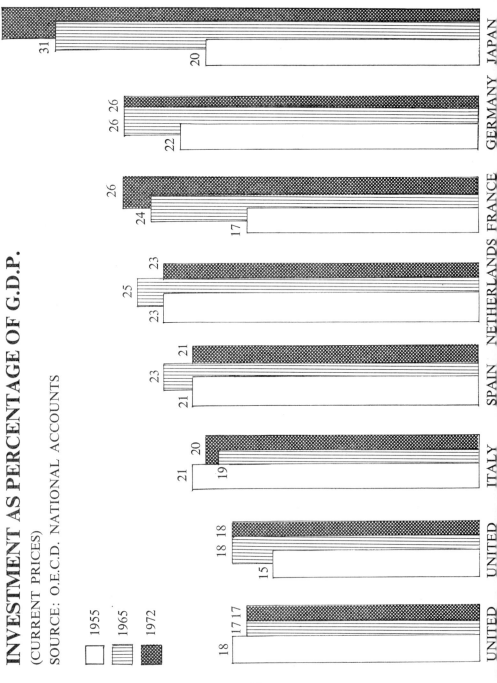

JAPAN

31

20

GERMANY

26 26

22

FRANCE

26

24

17

NETHERLANDS

23

25

23

SPAIN

21

23

21

ITALY

20

21

19

UNITED

18 18

15

UNITED

17 17

18

CHART X

SOURCE: OECD

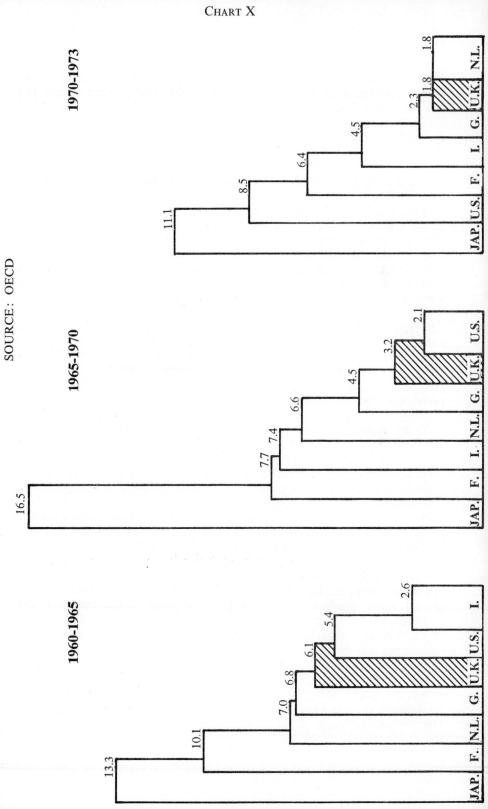

1960-1965

13.3 | JAP.
10.1 | F. N.L.
7.0 | G.
6.8 |
6.1 | U.K. U.S.
5.4 |
2.6 | I.

1965-1970

16.5 | JAP.
7.7 | F.
7.4 | I. N.L.
6.6 |
4.5 | G.
3.2 | U.K.
2.1 | U.S.

1970-1973

11.1 | JAP. U.S.
8.5 |
6.4 | F. I.
4.5 |
2.3 | G.
1.8 | U.K.
1.8 |
1.8 | N.L.

The main reason for the low increase in industrial output has been the very low rate of investment within Britain over recent years. Compared to other countries, British investment as a percentage of gross domestic product (Chart IX) has been far below that in all other developed countries except the United States. It has also increased more slowly (Chart X), at a 6.1 per cent average from 1960 to 1965, at 3.2 per cent from 1965 to 1970, and 1.8 per cent from 1970 to 1973. The United Kingdom has now the lowest rate of capital investment per employee of any major industrial country. Of the six largest industrial countries, the UK is the sixth in consumption of machine tools per employee*. As regards the age of machine tools, in Japan 62 per cent of all machine tools are less than ten years old. In Germany the figure is 56 per cent. In the UK only 38 per cent of the machine tools are less than a decade old. If this age profile is turned into relative manufacturing advantage (lower direct labour costs, reduction in setting-up time, reduced scrap, etc), then, it can be calculated that the industrial users of machine tools in Germany and Japan have an advantage of roughly 15 per cent to 20 per cent over British manufacturers†.

Low investment has been the result of the stop-go policies of the various British governments. The "stop" phase of the cycle, marked by restrictive monetary policy, wage freeze, credit squeezes etc. has served to curtail investment and production; the "go" phase has unfortunately been focused on consumer-led expansion rather than a selective promotion of productive investment. Deflation has damaged the British economy in three major ways:

(1) By repressing home demand, deflationary measures have dampened business expectations and confidence. As investment seemed less profitable the expansion of productive capacity has fallen.
(2) By monetary restraint making it more difficult for business to raise money on the stock market, more costly to get funds from banks, and less profitable to borrow.
(3) By creating a general climate of uncertainty, deflationary action has made it difficult for business to visualise future demand and sales and hence to commit the necessary funds to avoid investment slumps.

Not only has investment been low over past years in Britain, but the quality of the investment has been poorer than in other industrialised countries. As a general result, productivity (output per man-hour) in the manufacturing industries has risen very slowly—far more slowly than in any other country of Europe, as illustrated in Chart XI. The absolute value of productivity (output per man-hour in the economy as a whole) was already lower in Britain in 1969 than in other countries. From 1969 on, the gap has been widening.

---

*Consumption of machine tools means home output plus imports, minus exports.
†*The Times*, 21.12.1973.

TABLE 1

**Productivity per Man-hour in 1969**
(in US dollars at current price and exchange rates)

| | |
|---|---|
| United Kingdom .. .. | 1.68 |
| France.. .. .. .. | 2.43 |
| Italy .. .. .. .. | 1.75 |
| Netherlands .. .. .. | 2.59 |
| Germany .. .. .. | 2.46 |
| USA .. .. .. .. | 5.80 |
| Japan .. .. .. .. | 1.32 |

*Source:* EEC Data

CHART XI

# INDEX OF OUTPUT PER MAN HOUR (1967 = 100)

Source: MONTHLY LABOUR REVIEW NOVEMBER 1973

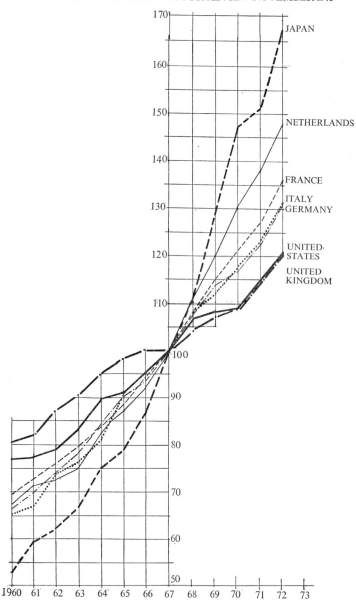

**Britain's foreign trade performance**

Britain is foremost a trader nation, and the international market has provided invaluable benefits to the country. Traditionally, this role in world commerce has brought not only profits for traders buying cheap in one market and selling dear in another, but it has given the country much of its economic vigour as well as certain of its political characteristics.

In centuries past Britain seldom lacked competitors, but in the twentieth century competition for world markets has become much more intensive as well as extensive. Strong new trader nations entered the field. In theory, more competition is supposed to invigorate an economy, with inefficiency penalised and the rewards of excellence enlarged. Unprofitable firms become competitive or go out of business, and the national economy therefore benefits.

Moving from theory to reality, and looking at the last 15 years, we find that in Britain what was supposed to happen did not happen. Increased competition brought no significant increases in competitiveness. In fact, during these fifteen years Britain's position in the international economy eroded significantly. This pronounced deterioration in competitiveness must be seen as one major cause for the decline of British economic strength. This conclusion emerges strongly from a comparison of Britain's recent experience with that of other industrialised and industrialising countries.

During the 1960's and early 1970's wage increases have been a major component in the rising costs of the manufacturing process in industrialised countries. Wage rises, as such, do not seriously affect a country's competitive position if they are accompanied by corresponding rises in productivity. This has not been the case in Great Britain in recent years.

Wage increases in Great Britain during the 1960's were sizeable, but still smaller than in some of Britain's main competitor countries. So far in the 1970's wage increases in the UK have been larger but not significantly more sizeable than elsewhere. In absolute terms, wages remain low in Britain.

TABLE 2
**Hourly Wages in Manufacturing**
(average annual increase in percentages)

|  |  |  |  | 1962–65 | 1965–69 | 1970–73 |
|---|---|---|---|---|---|---|
| United Kingdom | .. | .. | .. | 4.2 | 6.0 | 11.7 |
| France .. | .. | .. | .. | .. | 7.4 | 8.9 | 11.4 |
| Germany | .. | .. | .. | .. | 7.8 | 5.9 | 11.3 |
| Italy .. | .. | .. | .. | .. | 12.0 | 5.0 | 17.3 |
| United States .. | .. | .. | .. | 3.1 | 5.2 | 6.2 |
| Japan* .. | .. | .. | .. | .. | 9.7 | 14.0 | 17.6 |

* Monthly earnings
Source: OECD Main Economic Indicators

25

But as we have seen earlier, productivity increases consistently have been low. It is these two factors taken together—higher wage costs and low productivity increases—that have brought about a damaging change in unit labour costs. Table 3 measures the relative movement of productivity and wages: a rise in unit labour costs indicates that wage increases are outpacing productivity, and it is therefore the best indicator of comparable production cost trends in manufacturing. From this table it is clear that in the late 1960's and especially in the early 1970's unit labour costs increased greatly. Of our sample countries only Italy shows a worse performance.

TABLE 3
**Unit Labour Cost in Manufacturing***
(average annual increase in percentages)

|  | 1962–65 | 1965–69 | 1970–73 |
|---|---|---|---|
| United Kingdom .. .. .. | 2.1 | 2.7 | 8.1 |
| France .. .. .. .. .. | 3.4 | 2.2 | 6.3 |
| Germany .. .. .. .. | 2.6 | 1.4 | 7.5 |
| Italy .. .. .. .. .. | 5.7 | 1.9 | 11.4† |
| United States .. .. .. .. | −0.8 | 3.6 | 2.4 |
| Japan .. .. .. .. .. | 5.0 | 0.8 | 6.0 |

*Expressed in national currency.
†1970–72.
*Source:* International Economic Report of the President, Washington 1974.

Certainly the productivity of labour is strongly influenced by capital investment. More modern technology helps labour to produce more during a given period of time and dampens the labour cost of a unit of output. We have already seen that investment has lagged in the United Kingdom. Nevertheless, labour's relatively poor performance cannot be entirely blamed on the slow introduction (or the absence) of improved technology. The productivity of labour has also been strongly and negatively influenced by the high number of working days lost due to employment disputes.

Italy has a bad reputation internationally for time lost due to strikes, but in fact Britain has not done much better in recent years. If we look at the total number of working days lost in relation to the total civilian labour force, in three sample years the United Kingdom emerges as a country which is second only to Italy in time lost due to labour disputes. The difference between the two countries is small, especially in the year 1972. France and the United States are in a somewhat better situation (the figures for France in 1968 are not available, but undoubtedly are extremely high due to the national disruptions in May of that year). Japan, the Netherlands, Germany and Spain are in a much better position (the last-named for obvious political reasons).

26

CHART XII

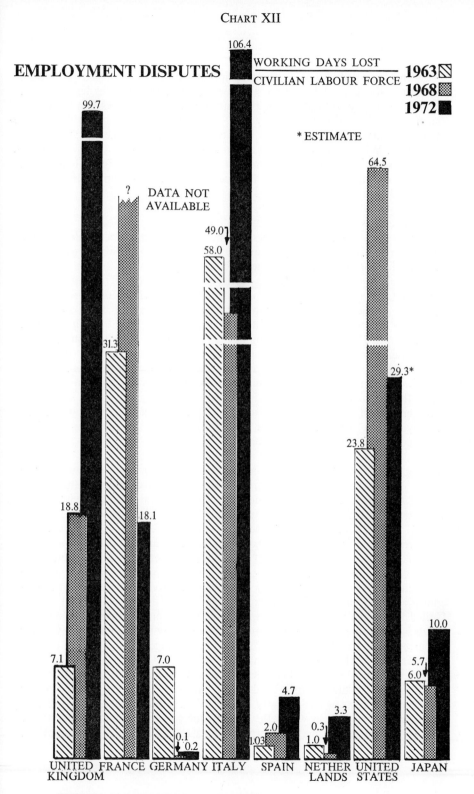

EMPLOYMENT DISPUTES

$\dfrac{\text{WORKING DAYS LOST}}{\text{CIVILIAN LABOUR FORCE}}$

1963
1968
1972

* ESTIMATE

DATA NOT AVAILABLE

106.4
99.7
?
58.0
49.0
64.5
31.3
29.3*
23.8
18.8
18.1
7.1
7.0
4.7
5.7
6.0
10.0
3.3
2.0
1.03
0.3
1.0
0.1
0.2

UNITED KINGDOM  FRANCE  GERMANY  ITALY  SPAIN  NETHER LANDS  UNITED STATES  JAPAN

SOURCE: ILO STATISTICAL YEARBOOK

27

The trend from 1963 to 1972, shows employment disputes consistently on the increase in the United Kingdom. In other nations, this trend is less obvious, except that it may be noted that the number of working days lost showed a sharp and sudden rise in the early 1970's in two countries where this phenomenon has traditionally been low or even negligible since the war: Germany and Spain. With changing labour attitudes in Germany—the years of labour deference seem to be finished—figures are expected to increase in the late 1970's. The same will undoubtedly be true for Spain with the relaxation of strict labour laws which presently forbid strikes.

**The competitive position**
Relatively low productivity increases and increasing labour costs in maufacturing would burden any industrialised country, but the effects are worse, overall, on the UK than on most other advanced economies because of the extraordinary importance of the manufacturing sector in this country. This can best be illustrated with so-called *snowflake* diagrams (Chart XIII). In *snowflakes* drawn for eight countries, the percentages of the civilian labour force employed in various sectors and subsectors of the economies are plotted along the arms of each chart. If, for example, a country were to show a *snowflake* shaped as a perfect hexagon, this would mean that each of the six sectors and subsectors plotted would employ one-sixth of the total working population. In the *snowflakes* given on our chart, Great Britain is revealed to have an economy where the secondary or manufacturing sector is extremely important: it employs 44.4 per cent of the total labour force. The primary sector is very small, and employment in the tertiary sector is concentrated in the *services*—banking, insurance, the liberal professions, etc.

A large industrial sector in an advanced economy is certainly not an intrinsic sign of bad economic health. Comparing the *snowflake* diagram of the UK to that of Germany, it is clear that industry in the Federal Republic employs an even larger part of the working population, 50.4 per cent, or 6 per cent more than Great Britain. There is, however, a major difference to be noted. The industrial sector in Germany is extremely efficient and modern. This is not true in the UK. An indication of the difference between these countries is found in the following table which compares the shares of employment and the contribution made to the GDP by the different productive sectors. In such countries as Germany, France, Japan, and the Netherlands, as well as the United States, the percentage of employees in the manufacturing (or secondary) sector is lower than the contribution actually made by the manufacturing sector in percentage terms to the GDP. In the United Kingdom, the reverse is true: 44.4 per cent of the people are employed in a sector which contributes only 42.7 per cent to the GDP. This means that industry is fairly labour-intensive in Britain. This situation may be desirable, at least temporarily, in a country with low wage costs, where industry is developing, but it is definitely undesirable in a country like Britain where the unit labour cost increases are consistently high and at the same time productivity increases are low. It is also important

28

TABLE 4
**Employment and Origin of GDP by Sector**
**1972**

| | United Kingdom | France | Germany | Italy | Spain | Netherlands | USA | Japan |
|---|---|---|---|---|---|---|---|---|
| EMPLOYMENT | | | | | | | | |
| Primary sector .. | 1·9 | 12·9 | 7·5 | 18·0 | 27·7 | 6·7 | 4·3* | 15·9* |
| Secondary sector .. | 44·4 | 40·3 | 50·4 | 43·8 | 37·2 | 35·9 | 31·0* | 36·0* |
| Tertiary sector .. | 53·5 | 46·8 | 41·9 | 38·2 | 35·1 | 57·4 | 64·7 | 48·1* |
| ORIGIN OF GDP | | | | | | | | |
| Primary sector .. | 2·9 | 6·0* | 2·9 | 8·0 | 12·8 | 5·3 | 3·0 | 6·0* |
| Secondary sector .. | 42·7 | 48·4 | 52·4 | 41·6 | 35·0 | 44·9 | 33·6 | 44·5* |
| Tertiary sector .. | 54·4 | 45·6* | 44·6 | 50·4 | 52·2 | 49·8 | 63·4 | 49·6* |

*1971 figures.
*Source:* ILO and OECD.

to note that even an efficient secondary sector can bring problems in a developed economy if this sector is emphasized too long and too heavily in the diagram. A recent study† by the respected World Economic Institute (Weltwirtschafts-institut) in Kiel has pointed out that an industrialising economy typically increases the weight of its manufacturing sector until a certain *per capita* income is reached whereupon economic stimuli emerge which tend to impede further growth in this sector or even decrease its importance—especially in terms of the number of people employed. That is, as people become wealthier, the demand for manufactured goods does not increase at a correspondingly rapid rate, but the demand for goods and services in the tertiary (services) sector increases. The Institute, addressing a West German audience, warned that policies which helped, and to some extent still help, maintain a large industrial employment sector in Germany can make structural adjustment much more difficult for Germany in the near future.

But it is not at all clear that conditions in the UK favour a decrease in the GDP share of the industrial sector to the benefit of certain parts of the tertiary sector. The tertiary sector as a whole is already quite large. It is, however, certain that to have a large percentage of the population employed in a sector of the economy which in important respects is inefficient, with obsolescent plant and equipment, is a very bad policy for the present and indicates substantial trouble in the future.

Inflation is a very important determinant of how a country competes inter-nationally. Inflation is usually discussed in terms of how it cuts into or even

---

†*Sektorale und Regionale Strukturprobleme der Westdeutschen Wirtschaft,* Die Weltwirtschafts-institut 1974-Heft 1 Kiel, Germany.

eliminates real wage increases. It must be emphasised that a country with high inflation rates must not only worry about how this directly affects the domestic economy but also how it affects the nation's competitive situation internationally. Regardless of the identifiable causes of inflation—be they higher import prices, higher wage costs, or excess demand conditions, or a combination of all—to suffer from a higher rate of inflation than one's competitors means disadvantage in the international marketplace. The table below illustrates how Britain is rapidly losing any competitive advantage it may once have enjoyed over certain other countries due to relatively low inflation rates.

TABLE 5
**Consumer Price**
(average annual increase in percentages)

|              | 1962–66 | 1966–69 | 1969–73 |
| ------------ | ------- | ------- | ------- |
| USA          | 1.4     | 3.8     | 4.9     |
| Japan        | 6.2     | 4.9     | 7.6     |
| West Germany | 2.9     | 2.4     | 5.4     |
| France       | 3.9     | 4.1     | 6.1     |
| UK           | 3.6     | 4.1     | 8.0     |
| Italy        | 5.6     | 2.4     | 6.3     |

*Source:* OECD.

Looking at the prospects for Britain's competitiveness over the remaining years of the decade, the forecast is rather gloomy. A country which has an important dependence upon labour-intensive industry cannot live for long with small productivity increases and rapidly increasing labour costs. Productivity must rise sharply by means of increases in technology, labour performance, or both. For Britain to try to keep wage increases to a minimum may be a logical endeavour but this will certainly be very difficult to achieve in the years to come, especially in view of the overall conditions of relative decline in living standards. A country with 84 per cent of its exports made up of manufactured products cannot afford an inefficient secondary sector. But this is what Britain has today. To maintain or regain competitiveness, cost advantages, reliability, and innovation are needed. Britain today is falling behind in all three respects.

**The British trade deficit**
Britain has run a trade deficit throughout its history. In this century, Britain has had 69 deficits and only four surpluses (1956, 1958, 1970 and 1971). This record has prompted considerable debate on the causes of consistent deficits, and the significance, if any, of these deficits for a nation which has been a *rentier* economy since the late 19th century, bringing the current account into balance or surplus by its earnings on invisibles.

Traditionally, the publication of adverse trade figures sent a shudder through the exchange markets and prompted an outflow of funds from London, forcing the authorities (under a regime of fixed rates) into considerable and costly exchange support of the pound. In the 1950's and early 1960's devaluation of the pound, a key currency, was unthinkable. Defence of the prestige of sterling and of the reputation of the City was responsible for much of the unhappy stop-go saga of postwar economic policy. Tory governments historically have been those attaching the greatest importance to the international roles of the City and the pound. As in the 1920's, when Winston Churchill, Chancellor of the Exchequer, took the decision to return sterling to its prewar parity while other nations devalued, the modern Tories have seemed more concerned with the prestige and earnings of the City's institutions than with renovating Britain's antiquated industrial structure. J. M. Keynes remarked in the 1920's that the British worker and British industry have consistently been sacrificed on the altar of high finance. In the interwar years, the Bank of England, the Treasury and most City financiers believed that the City could do more for the British economy than the whole of British industry and its exports—a view which is still widely held today. Labour's leaders, on the other hand, have usually tried to move in the direction of a competitive pound and a strong trade performance. It was the Labour government which took the emotion-charged step of devaluing the pound in 1967.

Much of the blame for the trade deficits of recent years has been placed on price and wage inflation in Britain, and these are said to have reduced the competitive position of British exports in third markets. The evidence on price and wage trends does not entirely support this conclusion. In the early sixties, as we have already seen, consumer prices, hourly wages, and unit labour costs rose somewhat less than in the main European countries. By the late sixties, however, Britain had caught up with the European average increase and from 1970 onwards was in the lead, and the trend was reflected in export prices (in national currencies) which from 1968 onwards rose faster than in the other major industrialised countries. Other commonly-stated reasons for Britain's poor export performance include old technology, a stagnant pattern of exports (i.e. failure to shift to new, expanding markets), production of the wrong goods (those with declining demand), the poor British reputation for prompt and reliable delivery and servicing, poor management and troubled labour relations. Whatever the reason, or complex of reasons, in the sixties British exports grew at two-thirds the pace of world trade. Britain's share of world exports fell from 8.2 per cent in 1960 to 7.3 per cent in 1965 and to 4.8 per cent in 1973, while the EEC's share rose from 33 per cent of world exports to 41 per cent in 1973. British exports in the sixties continued to be orientated towards the Commonwealth. Of total British exports, those to the Nine represented only 32 per cent as late as 1973, as against 55 per cent and 47 per cent shares in trade to the Nine for France and Germany.

# SNOWFLAKE DIAGRAMS FOR SELECTED COUNTRIES 1972

SOURCE: ILO STATISTICAL YEARBOOK

CHART XIII

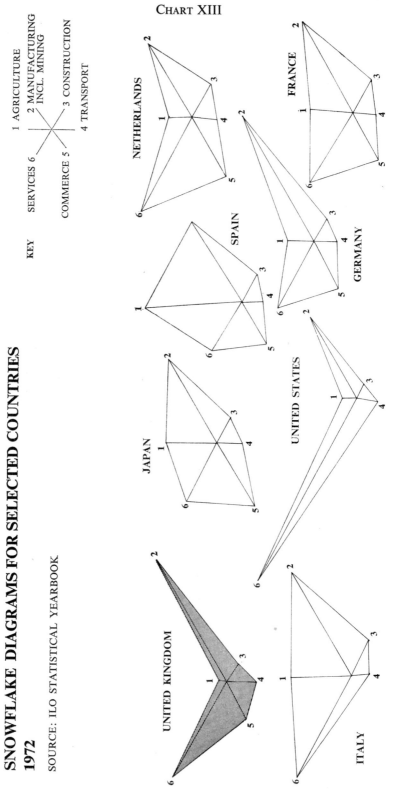

KEY

1 AGRICULTURE
2 MANUFACTURING INCL. MINING
3 CONSTRUCTION
4 TRANSPORT
COMMERCE 5
SERVICES 6

NETHERLANDS
FRANCE
SPAIN
GERMANY
JAPAN
UNITED STATES
UNITED KINGDOM
ITALY

## TABLE 6

### Direction of Exports (current dollars)
in percentage of total exports

| | United Kingdom | | France | | Germany | |
|---|---|---|---|---|---|---|
| | 1960 | 1973 | 1960 | 1973 | 1960 | 1973 |
| France .. .. .. | 3 | 5 | — | — | 9 | 13 |
| Germany .. .. | 5 | 6 | 14 | 19 | — | — |
| Italy .. .. .. | 3 | 3 | 6 | 12 | 6 | 8 |
| Benelux.. .. .. | 2 | 5 | 7 | 11 | 6 | 8 |
| Netherlands .. .. | 3 | 5 | 3 | 5 | 9 | 10 |
| United Kingdom .. | — | — | 5 | 6 | 4 | 5 |
| The Nine .. .. | 21 | 32 | 36 | 55 | 38 | 47 |
| The Six .. .. | 15 | 25 | 30 | 47 | 30 | 40 |
| US .. .. .. | 7 | 12 | 6 | 5 | 8 | 8 |
| USSR .. .. .. | 1 | 1 | 2 | 2 | 2 | 2 |
| Developing Countries.. | 32 | 21 | 40 | 20 | 19 | 12 |
| Latin America .. | 4 | 3 | 4 | 2 | 6 | 3 |
| Africa .. .. .. | 8 | 5 | 29 | 9 | 3 | 3 |
| Middle East .. .. | 5 | 6 | 3 | 3 | 4 | 3 |

*Source:* IMF: Direction of Trade.

The composition of British exports is also changing (Table 13). Manufactured goods continue to account for 84 per cent of British exports, but among them capital goods (machinery)—which used to be major British exports, symbolising superiority of British technology, are in decline. The opposite trend can be observed in Germany where exports of capital goods are becoming dominant; they are now 48 per cent of total German exports. This slowing of British capital goods exports has been accompanied by a rise in imports in this same category. Capital goods were 10 per cent of total imports in 1960 but 20 per cent in 1972. Britain seems increasingly dependent on the outside world for goods it used to export.

The British trade deficit owes much to a rapid rise in imports overall since the early 1970's; a rise both in volume and price. Between 1966 and 1971 the volume of imports grew three times as fast as output, and in late 1972, the growth was three-and-a-half times as fast. According to the Bank of England, over the past twelve years Britain has experienced a rise in imports of manufactures of some 16 per cent per year. Manufactured goods now account for 55 per cent of total British imports (in 1972) against only 43 per cent in 1960. For capital goods the change was a doubling between 1960 and 1972. This trend was especially obvious at the end of 1973 when in response to shortages and stock-building at home, British imports of semi-manufactured goods rose by 50 per cent in a single quarter.

CHART XIV

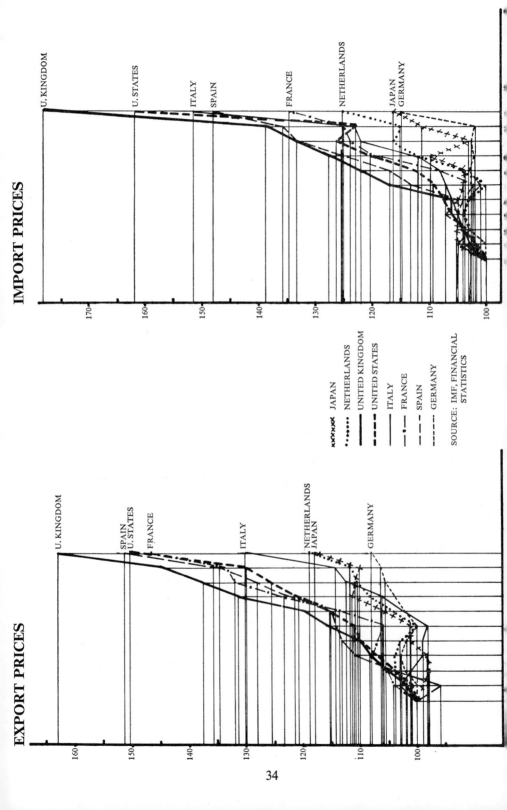

34

The increased volume of imports was accompanied by a rise in the price of imports (Chart XIV), and British imports unfortunately are peculiarly price inelastic. That is to say Britain needs them and thus is in a poor position to cut down on imports when prices go up. Foodstuffs and primary goods are an important part of total British imports, and these have to be imported at any cost. British industry is also increasingly dependent on imports. Each time the British government has gone on an export drive to re-establish the balance of trade, British firms, in order to produce more for export, have had to increase their imports of capital goods. Any rise in exports thus brings a rise in imports. This is because of the lack of investment in British industry in the past, a point which we will discuss elsewhere.

### Invisible earnings

Britain's trade performance is not the same as its overall performance in balancing payments with foreign countries. The country earns a great deal in invisibles. These include such earnings from foreign insurance and investment earnings, tourism, and services generally. The current account was in surplus during the 1960's except for the years 1964, 1965, 1967 and 1968. Trade deficits were offset by a steadily growing surplus on invisibles. Looking at the invisibles accounts (see Table 7), earnings in the private sector have steadily increased, especially in the service category including transport, banking and insurance. In earlier years, interest, profits and dividends on direct and portfolio investment abroad constituted the largest single component in the surplus, contributing nearly twice the earnings on services and transfers. Since 1969, this category has fallen considerably below earnings on the other two sectors and, for many economists, the increasing importance of services in the national and external accounts is a natural development. As economies mature, a proportionally smaller part of the labour force is engaged in manufacturing, freeing labour and capital for the development of sophisticated services of all kinds. But it seems to us that this argument is a dangerous and misleading one to apply to Britain's invisible trade. These invisible earnings from abroad follow from British investments abroad, and Britain always has been and remains a heavy exporter of capital. It seems clear to us that this foreign investment has, in fact, penalised Britain's own domestic economy. British foreign investment has occurred at the expense of home investment, and the result has been to leave British industry outmoded and uncompetitive, the economy dangerously vulnerable to political and economic uncertainty abroad.

35

## TABLE 7

### UK Current Account 1963-73
million pounds

| | 1963 | 1964 | 1965 | 1966 | 1967 | 1968 | 1969 | 1970 | 1971 | 1972 | 1973 |
|---|---|---|---|---|---|---|---|---|---|---|---|
| **1) Visible Trade** | | | | | | | | | | | |
| Exports .. .. .. .. .. | 4282 | 4486 | 4817 | 5184 | 5124 | 6274 | 7063 | 7893 | 8790 | 9134 | 11435 |
| Imports .. .. .. .. .. | 4362 | 5005 | 5054 | 5257 | 5681 | 6922 | 7206 | 7881 | 8491 | 9819 | 13810 |
| Balance .. .. .. .. .. | −80 | −519 | −237 | −73 | −557 | −648 | −143 | +12 | +299 | −685 | −2375 |
| **2) Invisibles** | | | | | | | | | | | |
| a) Gov. Serv. & Trans. .. .. | −382 | −432 | −447 | −470 | −463 | −466 | −467 | −486 | −527 | −548 | −790 |
| b) Other Private Serv. & Trans... | +188 | +176 | +200 | +200 | +240 | +508 | +557 | +661 | +798 | +948 | +860 |
| c) Int., Profits, Dividends: | | | | | | | | | | | |
| Private .. .. .. .. | +531 | +512 | +569 | +546 | +551 | +571 | +831 | +756 | +669 | +623 | +1280 |
| Public .. .. .. .. | −133 | −119 | −134 | −159 | −172 | −236 | −334 | −262 | −199 | −147 | −195 |
| Balance .. .. .. .. | +204 | +137 | +188 | +157 | +242 | +377 | +587 | +669 | +741 | +768 | +1165 |
| **3) Current Account** .. .. | +124 | −382 | −49 | +84 | −315 | −271 | +444 | +681 | +1040 | +83 | −1210 |

*Source:* Central Statistical Office, United Kingdom Balance of Payments, 1972, 1973.

The problems inherent in this British penchant for sending capital abroad instead of nourishing British industry at home can be seen by two key comparisons. In the United States, the other key *rentier* economy, earnings on interest, profits and dividends have exceeded net new capital outflows since 1958. In other words, there has been no net loss to the economy. In Britain, however, since 1968, net new outflow has tended to exceed earnings on this investment, as the following tables reveal:

### TABLE 8
### British Investments and Earnings Abroad
million pounds

| | 1963 | 1964 | 1965 | 1966 | 1967 | 1968 | 1969 | 1970 | 1971 | 1972 | 1973 |
|---|---|---|---|---|---|---|---|---|---|---|---|
| UK private long-term capital (−) | 320 | 399 | 368 | 303 | 456 | 727 | 679 | 773 | 875 | 1472 | 1382 |
| Interest, profits, dividends (+) | 531 | 512 | 569 | 546 | 551 | 571 | 831 | 756 | 669 | 623 | 1290 |
| Balance | 211 | 113 | 201 | 243 | 95 | −186 | 159 | −17 | −206 | −849 | −92 |

The comparison between investment and earnings abroad supports the argument that Britain not only is not profiting from its foreign investment but is also investing abroad beyond its means. Until the First World War, Britain's strong industrial base and high invisible earnings provided the means to invest abroad. The surplus on current account was not converted but re-invested abroad. For most of the 1960's and 1970's, however, long-term investment exceeded the current account surplus (with the notable exception of 1971, which saw a record trade and current account surplus).

### TABLE 9
### Foreign Investment and Earnings
million pounds

| | 1963 | 1965 | 1968 | 1970 | 1971 | 1972 | 1973 |
|---|---|---|---|---|---|---|---|
| Current account surplus | 124 | −49 | −271 | 681 | 1040 | 83 | −1210 |
| Long-term private foreign investment | −320 | −368 | −727 | −773 | −875 | −1472 | −1382 |
| Excess investment over CA surplus | −196 | −417 | −998 | −92 | +165 | −1389 | −2592 |

37

## TABLE 10

### UK Capital Account and Official Financing
million pounds

| | | INVESTMENT AND OTHER CAPITAL FLOWS | | | | | | | | | | | OTHER OFFICIAL FINANCING (b) | | | |
|---|---|---|---|---|---|---|---|---|---|---|---|---|---|---|---|---|
| | Govt. long-term capital | Private Investment | | Trade Credit | | Overseas Sterling reserves | | Banks' borrowing in NSA currencies | Miscellaneous | Total | Adjustment items (a) | Net assistance | | Reserves (c) | Total |
| | | In UK | By UK | Imports | Exports | Sterling area | Other countries | | | | | IMF | Other | | |
| 1963 | − 105 | + 270 | − 320 | + 26 | − 115 | + 119 | + 2 | − 11 | + 35 | − 99 | — | + 5 | — | + 53 | − 58 |
| 1964 | − 116 | + 158 | − 399 | + 2 | − 48 | + 32 | − 53 | + 161 | − 38 | − 301 | — | + 357 | + 216 | + 122 | + 695 |
| 1965 | − 85 | + 226 | − 368 | + 6 | − 52 | − 68 | − 82 | + 22 | + 119 | − 326 | — | + 489 | + 110 | − 246 | + 353 |
| 1966 | − 81 | + 299 | − 303 | − 6 | − 198 | − 71 | + 42 | + 192 | − 68 | − 578 | + 272 | + 15 | + 294 | − 34 | + 275 |
| 1967 | − 59 | + 414 | − 456 | + 13 | − 193 | − 107 | − 81 | + 36 | − 62 | − 495 | + 230 | − 339 | + 691 | + 16 | + 336 |
| 1968 | + 16 | + 583 | − 727 | + 75 | − 321 | − 84 | − 96 | + 15 | − 187 | − 756 | − 251 | + 506 | + 790 | + 114 | +1410 |
| 1969 | − 99 | + 673 | − 679 | + 153 | − 325 | + 311 | + 3 | − 38 | − 108 | − 109 | — | + 30 | − 669 | − 44 | − 743 |
| 1970 | − 204 | + 715 | − 773 | + 17 | − 261 | + 183 | + 10 | + 472 | + 320 | + 479 | + 133 | − 134 | −1161 | − 125 | −1420 |
| 1971 | − 273 | +1187 | − 875 | + 77 | − 172 | + 506 | + 207 | + 499 | + 707 | +1863 | + 63 | − 554 | −1263 | −1348 | −3165 |
| 1972 | − 255 | + 834 | −1472 | + 187 | − 296 | + 329 | − 42 | + 471 | − 542 | − 786 | + 165 | − 172 | + 864 | + 408 | +1100 |
| 1973 | − 252 | +1752 | −1382 | + 128 | − 232 | | − 115 | +1217 | − 275 | +1071 | + 408 | — | — | − 210 | − 210 |

(a) Gold subscription to IMF, transfers to reserves from dollar portfolio, allocations of SDRs, valuation adjustments, including compensation payments under Sterling Agreements, and EEA losses on forward transactions.

(b) Valued at £1 = $2·60571 for quarters in 1972 and 1973 and annual figure for 1972; valued at £1 = $2·89524 for annual figure for 1973 and months in 1974.

(c) A plus sign denotes a fall and a minus sign a rise. The IMF reserve position is excluded.

*Source*: National Institute of Economic and Social Research, *National Institute Economic Review*, February 1974, and Central Statistical Office, *United Kingdom Balance of Payments*, 1972–3.

# CHART XV

**DIRECT INVESTMENTS ABROAD** (IN MILLION DOLLARS)

SOURCES: ONU, OECD (1972), BALANCE OF PAYMENTS
YEARBOOK (VARIOUS), INTERNATIONAL
MONETARY FUND

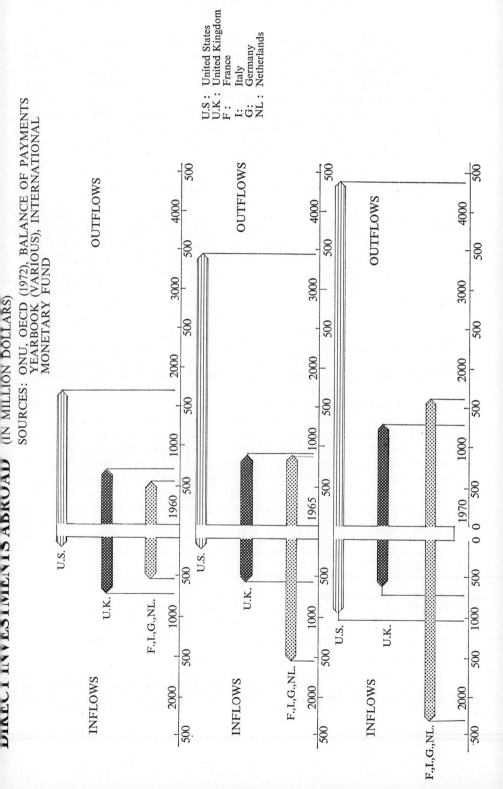

U.S : United States
U.K : United Kingdom
F : France
I : Italy
G : Germany
NL : Netherlands

39

As other analysts have observed, this ability to invest abroad in excess of earnings has been permitted only by Britain's privileged banking role. In effect, for most of this century Britain has been lending other people's money. In any given year, rather than demanding settlement of Britain's deficit, foreigners have invested their surplus sterling at short-term in the London market. Britain has continued to play the role of banker to the world, borrowing short and lending long, even when the domestic resources that once supported this lending have disappeared. The present pattern—relying essentially on foreign deposits in London to continue an ambitious investment policy abroad*—is remarkably similar to the interwar pattern, and would be extended by any sizeable inflow of investments from Arab oil-producing countries in years ahead.

During sterling's heyday as a reserve currency, this situation was understandable and acceptable. Sterling's universal acceptability as a means of payment, the desire of foreigners to maintain working balances in sterling, and the attraction of profits on this investment, all encouraged the deposit of these funds in London. As the British economy, and sterling's fortunes, have declined, the costs have become increasingly heavy. Under fixed parities, the authorities felt compelled to clamp down on the domestic economy severely and to intervene in the exchange markets to maintain the parity of sterling and thus keep foreign deposits in London. With a floating pound, it has been necessary to offer exchange guarantees. The cost has not been negligible—totalling an estimated £140 million since the beginning of 1973—and some countries, such as Australia, have begun to convert their sterling balances despite the guarantees.

The long-term difficulties of relying on foreign goodwill should not be discounted. Authorities still manage monetary policy in Britain with an eye to sterling's exchange quotations and foreign funds in London, even when restraint is not necessarily warranted by the state of the domestic economy. Britain has already experienced some of the perils of relying on foreign investment. Two major wars, forced liquidation of a substantial part of British foreign investment, and rising economic nationalism in the developing world are all testaments to the vulnerability of a *rentier* economy. As Friedrich List observed in the 19th century, the power of producing wealth is vastly more important than wealth itself. An economy which has relinquished its own productive power for reliance on earnings from abroad remains at the mercy of events and decisions beyond its control.

### Recent trends and prospects
In 1972, Britain experienced a severe deterioration in the trade accounts because of three major factors: a virtual stagnation of exports; a startling rise of 10 per cent in the volume of goods and services imported at a time when output rose

---

*British direct investments abroad are still far higher than any other European country taken individually, and only slightly less than France's, Germany's, Italy's and Netherlands' taken together (Chart XV).

by only 3 per cent; and a rapid increase in the cost of British imports, particularly of food and raw materials because of the commodities boom starting in mid-1972 and the depreciation of the floating pound. In 1972, the terms of trade (i.e. the ratio of export to import prices) moved against Britain by some 10 per cent. Although export prices rose by 18 per cent, import prices rose by 31 per cent and this price effect accounted for almost nine-tenths of the trade deterioration.*

There was general consensus that depreciation of the pound was a necessary corrective since British costs and prices, especially of exports, were rising faster than its competitors. Yet, in the short-run, deliberate depreciation by a country which depends on imports for food and raw materials at a time when prices are rising at an unprecedented rate, can only cause a severe deterioration in the trade balance. In short, political leaders could hardly blame Britain's trade troubles on events beyond their control.

On the invisible accounts, although government and private earnings on services and transfers increased, interest, profits and dividends fell, reducing invisible earnings. Because of this and the adverse trade swing, the current account fell from a £1 billion surplus to a meagre £83 million.

In 1973, a continuing boom in the prices of commodities and oil added to the problems of a depreciating currency and high domestic inflation. Under the influence of these price and exchange rate movements, the visible trade deficit increased every quarter for a record yearly deficit of £2·3 billion. Dearer oil, although a troublesome factor, was responsible for only a part of the deterioration. The big increase in Britain's 1973 import bill came from semi-manufactures, in response to shortages and stock building at home. Although invisibles reached a healthy £1,165 million, they were unable to offset a trade deficit almost two-and-a-half times as large, and the current account registered a deficit of some £1·2 billion.

This current account deficit was an ominous sign even before the spectacular increase in oil prices in December 1973. In the past, the current account surplus helped to finance private and official outflows. A heavy oil deficit to finance, in addition to the sizeable non-oil component, imposes a large increase in the government interest payments burden. In other words, invisibles will continue to decline, because of the government's financing costs, while the growing trade deficit shows little signs of amelioration.

Figures for the first half of 1974 (nearly £2 billion deficit) indicate that the current account deficit will be at least £4 billion and may be closer to £5 billion for 1974. The oil deficit has been running at an average monthly rate of £254 million or a yearly rate of £3 billion. Contrary to expectations, the non-oil

---

*Bank of England Quarterly Review, vol. 13, No. 14, Dec. 1973.

deficit has failed to improve and will probably total as much as £2 billion for 1974. In other words, the non-oil deficit accounts for over one-third of the current account deficit.

TABLE 11

**British Current Account**
**First Half 1974**
million pounds

*Visible Balance: Trade in Goods*

|  | Petroleum and petroleum products | Other Goods | Total | Current Account |
|---|---|---|---|---|
| January .. .. .. | −166 | −223 | −389 | −307 |
| February .. .. .. | −247 | −182 | −429 | −347 |
| March .. .. .. | −294 | −159 | −453 | −371 |
| April .. .. .. | −308 | −83 | −391 | −309 |
| May .. .. .. .. | — | — | — | — |
| June .. .. .. .. | — | — | −477 | −374 |
| Monthly average .. .. | −254 | −162 | −416 | −334 |
| Yearly rate .. .. .. | 3,048 | 1,944 | 4,992 | 4,008 |

Although the export volume of goods and services rose some 4.5 per cent in the first half of 1974, the trade deficit was far worse than expected, largely because of the increase in import prices. In the second quarter of the year, these were 60 per cent above their level a year earlier and twice their 1970 base level.*

British forecasting institutions expect the trade deficit, now running at an annual rate of £5 billion, to decline to £3.5 billion by the end of 1975, and the current account deficit to fall to only £2.7 billion in 1975—(and only £789 million for the non-oil deficit) despite the inescapable facts that domestic output is falling, prices and wages are accelerating, the oil bill is increasing, and domestic production of oil has been seriously delayed. Even the trade forecasts assume that Britain's exports will increase much more rapidly than imports, which are assumed to remain stable in volume.

---

*As Hudson Europe has pointed out in earlier analyses of the British trade situation, the expected turn-around in the trade account was based on hopes rather than realistic appraisal. Even at the beginning of the year it was easy to point out at least three major reasons for a continued trade deterioration this year. First, during the three-day week, much domestic and foreign demand was met from stocks. As these were replenished, much had to be supplied through imports. Second, total output actually fell by 2 per cent in the first quarter of 1974. Third, national inflation rates were rising rapidly. Nevertheless, in Britain the argument was commonly made that trade account difficulties came only from a higher than expected increase in the price of imports, sluggish world demand, and a loss in competitiveness through high inflation at home.

Thus the keystones of the government's policy, at present, are a major export drive—intended both to turn around the balance of payments and stimulate the domestic economy—and official borrowing to keep the country afloat until the North Sea oil comes ashore. There are, however, numerous obstacles in the way. Much depends on the price and income elasticity of British imports and exports. Much of the hoped-for reduction in the value of British imports has come from a fall in food and raw materials prices, not from any reduction in imports inspired by price changes. At the same time, exports seem to depend increasingly on the quality of the goods produced, on good distribution networks, on prompt and reliable servicing and deliveries—in short, on all those areas in which Britain in recent years has proved to be weak.

There is also a basic problem of just what Britain will export. Manufacturers, as we have seen, have been a stagnant component of exports but a rapidly rising component of imports. It seems much more likely therefore that an increase in investment and output will create an increase in imports, not the desired exports. The refusal or inability to recognise that investment and supply problems are at the heart of the British trade difficulty seems to be the signal failure of the 1960's and 1970's. Instead of concentrating on productive investment at home, on industrial renovation and re-organisation, on shifting resources from sectors with declining markets to those with expanding demand and markets, British leaders are following the age-old habit of blaming Britain's troubles on the outside world.

It is a significant sign of the state of British economic management that prime importance is still attached to exporting, in itself an essential activity but one lacking any real influence for structural change in the economy itself. While the stability of the currency and the ability to buy imports are linked to export performance, there has long been exaggerated emphasis on the export sector of the economy. Much post war policy for growth has been firmly tied to "export-led" stimulation, with a resulting emphasis on traditional manufacturing industries. For this reason, the motto "Export or Die" may contain the wrong conjunction: for it has guaranteed that Britain has maintained those manufacturing sectors often of greatest age or the most inefficient construction.

The policy-structures linked to "export-led" growth have reflected a generally held view of the economy as being primarily a manufacturer and trader of basic products: this therefore has encouraged many industries that should have been phased out, or, even more important, has led industrialists to believe that the measure of their success, and by implication their strength, is the volume of exports they could attain. In our view the "Queen's Award to Industry for Export Services" would far better have been made an award for technological innovation or for a particularly impressive performance in productivity. Strategies of growth geared to the development of all sectors, rather than only of those contributing to the trade balance, must evolve if the British economy is to break out of a circle of vulnerability to fluctuations in the international trade cycle, the parity of sterling, and the tariff policies of governments abroad.

43

**Britain's standard of living**
A discussion of the economic situation of the United Kingdom which makes comparisons with other countries certainly highlights the difficulties of the country, and its problems in the international marketplace, but there is a danger that economic data—whatever their practical implications—remain just figures to many readers. To talk about the problems of a low rate of growth may be interesting to scholars or journalists, but remote to the average man. The figures on low investment, low competitiveness, balance of payments surpluses or deficits, etc. have varying degrees of urgency to various groups, but for many people these issues do not really relate to their day-to-day problems.

To show that *per capita* GNP in the United Kingdom is very low and that the situation is deteriorating does deal with "real life", but the true day-to-day significance of living in a low-growth economy like Great Britain can be seen, perhaps more vividly, with several economic and social indicators that deal directly and urgently with the standard of living and the equality of life.

For example, despite the fact that wages in manufacturing have increased over recent years in Britain, this has not meant that real wage increases for the British worker have been large. During the 1960's in particular, even the nominal wage rises were rather low compared to many other countries. Wage earners in the United Kingdom found that their already relatively low salaries were not markedly improved in real terms because inflation took away much of what was seemingly gained. Consumer prices went up almost as fast as wages, and over the last fifteen years Britain has the worst, or the next to worst, record of all our countries. In Chart XVI average annual wage increases in the industrial countries are represented by bars which stand against others showing the rise in consumer prices during the same period. Not only are wage increases in the 1960's low but even the high wage increases of the early 1970's have not brought any improvement in *real* wages for the British workman and employee. People in other countries have done much better. Between 1960 and 1965 British workers were worse off than any of the workers in the other seven countries, and in the periods 1965–70 and 1970–73 only US workers (whose absolute level of wages are, of course, much higher) experienced lower increases in *real* wages.

Another matter of special concern is unemployment. A high level of unemployment is not a necessary consequence of a stagnant economy. Indeed, rapid economic growth can in some circumstances be accompanied by relatively high levels of unemployment. Much depends on the structure of the economy and the economic and social prorities of governmental policy. Nonetheless, in the long run, there is a direct relationship between the vigour and the flexibility of an economy and the percentage of people gainfully employed. And a high level of unemployment obviously means a major social problem in the country. There is a limit to what any government can do, and keeping down unemployment is one of the many objectives that must be reconciled—or traded off, against some other factor—in a government's policy. In a low-growth, low-investment, low-productivity, high inflation situation, a necessary and continuous preoccupation with the unemployment problem is a tremendous burden in making national economic policy. We find, looking at Chart XVII that unemployment was high in the United Kingdom all through the 1960's and early 1970's. Unemployment figures were higher still in the United States, but here a word of caution is needed. Official statistics in the United States are calculated in such a way that large groups of people are included that do not appear in the British statistics. As *The Economist* said recently, "On American definitions of 'looking for work', Britain's unemployment figures are actually . . . understatements . . . Probably what is called a $2\frac{1}{2}\%$ unemployment rate in Britain would be called something like a 5% unemployment rate in America and a $1\frac{1}{2}\%$ rate in Germany."*

**The "quality of life" in Britain**
The social implications of Britain's economic retardation are very widely underestimated. Only that can explain why, in some circles, there can be continuing optimism about the standard of living and quality of life in the United Kingdom. Certainly the postwar years have brought improving sanitary conditions and health care, a higher life expectancy and lower rate of infant mortality in Britain, more consumer goods and better dwellings, etc. But the truth of the matter is that things have not improved as much as they should have improved, and by these measures, the British people do not now live as well as people do in the advanced countries of Europe. To say this in Britain very often is to meet scepticism if not downright disbelief. The British people as a whole are accustomed to think of themselves as enjoying one of the highest living standards in the world. Even when they know—as many, especially in the middle and professional classes who travel extensively, do know—that the material comparisons are increasingly unfavourable, they console themselves by saying that the intangibles of life in Britain make living here better than life elsewhere. Intangibles, by definition, cannot be measured, and of course what is important to one man may not be to the next. So, we cannot attempt to compare the subtleties of the *good life* as it is led in Britain, France, or Spain. We will have to limit ourselves to a few of the things that can readily be measured.

In the most fundamental sense, quality of life means health and longevity. The British National Health Service was a great and pioneering measure in social legislation, and most Britons can be expected to believe that it has, over the last three decades, given the country a level of health better than that of the continent. The comparisons do not show that this is so. In Chart XVIII the absolute level as well as the changes in life expectancy are given for various countries. On the left are points representing the situation at the beginning of the 1950's. The average male Briton could expect to live to his mid-60's and the female life expectancy was 71·2. Only in the Netherlands was the situation

---

*The Economist,* 7-13 September, 1974.

CHART XVI

# HOURLY WAGES AND PRICE INCREASES

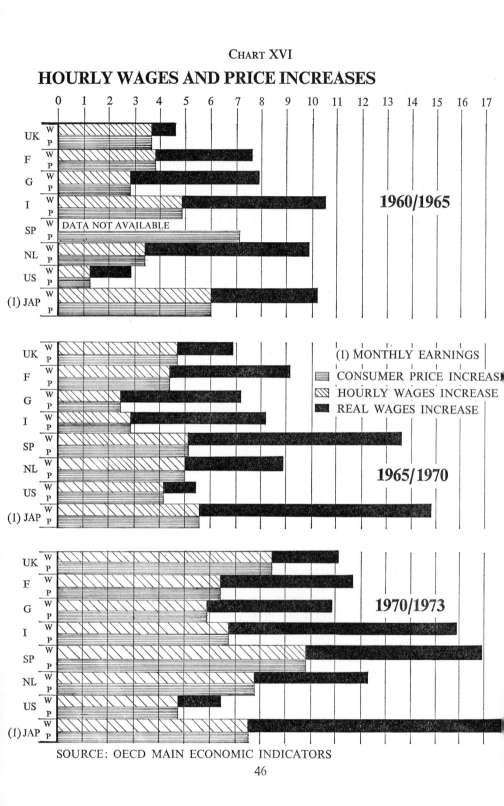

SP: DATA NOT AVAILABLE

1960/1965

(1) MONTHLY EARNINGS
CONSUMER PRICE INCREASE
HOURLY WAGES INCREASE
REAL WAGES INCREASE

1965/1970

1970/1973

SOURCE: OECD MAIN ECONOMIC INDICATORS

46

# UNEMPLOYMENT

SOURCE: ILO STATISTICAL YEARBOOK AND OECD MAIN ECONOMIC INDICATORS 1974

% OF TOTAL LABOUR FORCE

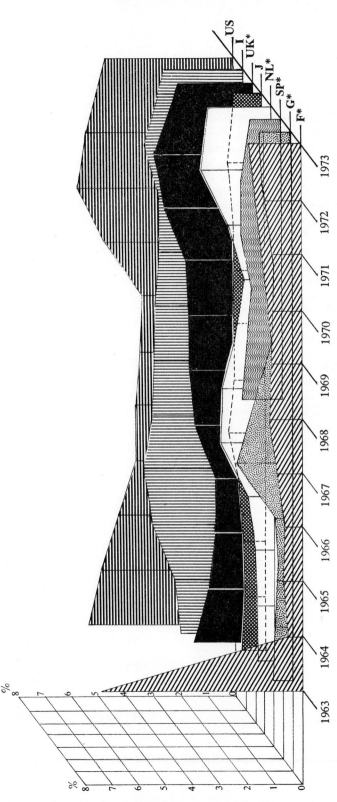

Chart XVII

* OFFICIALLY REGISTERED UNEMPLOYMENT ONLY

better. The graphs then show the general trend to the start of the 1970's. Within approximately twenty years, France, Japan and (probably) the United States had overtaken Great Britain. Germany, a country with a surprisingly poor showing in many statistics pertaining to public health, had virtually caught up with the United Kingdom. Since the figures for the United States date from 1966–68 rather than 1968–70 (as in the case of the United Kingdom), it is fair to assume that that country is better off today than the chart would indicate.

In Chart XIX, we make the same summary of statistics for infant mortality— i.e. the number of children who die at birth or shortly thereafter per thousand live births. Again, points representing the situation in 1950, 1960 and 1971 are connected by straight lines, and again the figures present an unfavourable picture for the United Kingdom. France, the Netherlands, and Japan most of all, have drastically reduced their infant mortality rates. The improvement in Germany is pronounced. Italy and the United States are still worse off than the UK but they are improving more rapidly.

Four other "quality of life" indicators are deemed important by the OECD: the number of dwellings completed, the number of doctors available per thousand inhabitants, and the number of passenger cars and telephones in a country. The latter two indicators show that Britain is well off in 'phones and private transportation. In housing construction, Britain shows poorly (Chart XX). In the number of doctors per thousand population, it is third from last on the OECD list. Such indicators do not in themselves prove the inferiority of conditions in the United Kingdom, but the two most important ones give added substance to the argument that as far as quality of life is measurable, it is less than satisfactory in a country that prides itself on having a special advantage in this respect.

CHART XVIII

# TRENDS IN LIFE EXPECTANCY

SOURCE: UNITED NATIONS YEAR BOOK

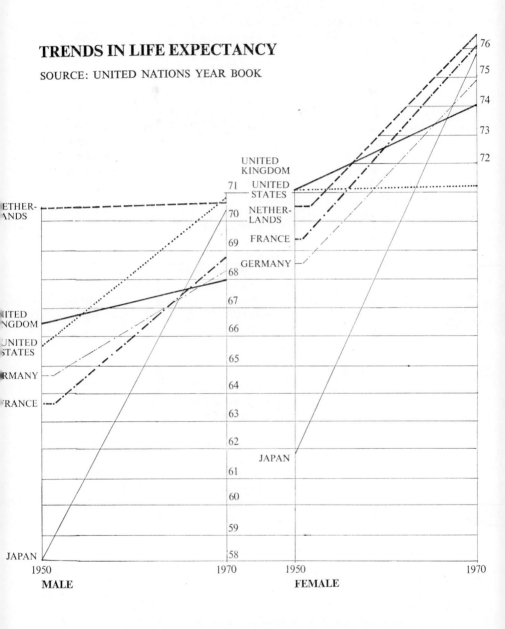

MALE                    FEMALE

TABLE 12
## Quality of Life Indicators

DOCTORS
  per 1000 inhabitants:

| Country | 1968 |
|---|---|
| Italy | 1·71 |
| Germany | 1·69* |
| United States | 1·49* |
| Spain | 1·34* |
| France | 1·18 |
| United Kingdom | 1·15 |
| Netherlands | 1·14 |
| Japan | 1·11* |

PASSENGER CARS
  per 1000 inhabitants:

| Country | 1971 |
|---|---|
| United States | 446 |
| France | 261 |
| Germany | 240 |
| United Kingdom | 219 |
| Netherlands | 212 |
| Italy | 210 |
| Japan | 101 |
| Spain | 82 |

NUMBER OF TELEPHONES
  per 1000 inhabitants:

| Country | 1971 |
|---|---|
| United States | 604 |
| United Kingdom | 289 |
| Japan | 282 |
| Netherlands | 280 |
| Germany | 249 |
| Italy | 188 |
| France | 185 |
| Spain | 151 |

---

*1969
*Source:* OECD
*Note:* Countries ranked in order of decreasing magnitude.

Chart XIX

# INFANT MORTALITY

SOURCE: U.N. STATISTICAL YEARBOOK 1972
RATE PER THOUSAND LIVE BIRTHS

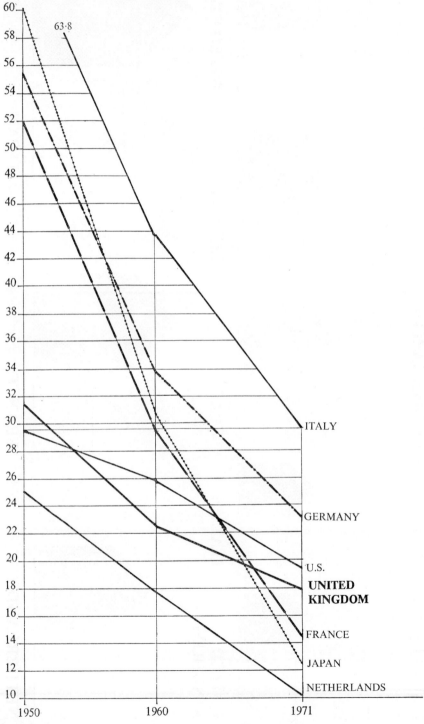

CHART XX

# DWELLINGS COMPLETED PER 1000 INHABITANTS

SOURCE: O.E.C.D. 1968 / 1971

1968
1971

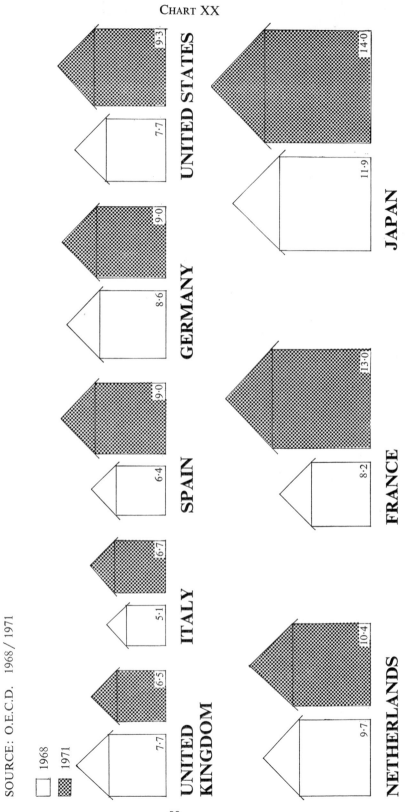

UNITED STATES

9·3
7·7

GERMANY

9·0
8·6

SPAIN

9·0
6·4

ITALY

6·7
5·1

UNITED KINGDOM

6·5
7·7

JAPAN

14·0
11·9

FRANCE

13·0
8·2

NETHERLANDS

10·4
9·7

## TABLE 13
### COMPOSITION OF TRADE
**Imports by Commodities—1960/1972**
(percentage of total imports)

|  |  | France | G'many | Italy | Neth. | U.K. | U.S.A. | Japan | Spain |
|---|---|---|---|---|---|---|---|---|---|
| Foods and live | 1960 | 15·0 | 21·4 | 15·3 | 12·3 | 30·7 | 20·4 | * | * |
| animals | 1972 | 10·9 | 15·3 | 19·6 | 11·7 | 18·8 | 10·5 | 14·6 | 10·8 |
| Beverage and | 1960 | 5·2 | 1·7 | 0·5 | 1·6 | 3·2 | 2·7 | * | * |
| tobacco | 1972 | 1·3 | 1·6 | 0·9 | 1·4 | 2·3 | 1·7 | 0·7 | 1·6 |
| Crude | 1960 | 22·9 | 22·6 | 27·5 | 13·4 | 10·6 | 10·8 | * | * |
| materials | 1972 | 8·9 | 10·5 | 13·9 | 7·9 | 11·1 | 14·3 | 30·3 | 17·3 |
| Mineral | 1960 | 17·2 | 7·8 | 14·1 | 13·1 | 10·6 | 10·8 | * | * |
| fuel | 1972 | 13·2 | 9·2 | 15·1 | 13·2 | 11·1 | 7·9 | 24·4 | 14·4 |
| Animal and | 1960 | 0·8 | 1·5 | 2·8 | 1·5 | 1·2 | 0·7 | * | * |
| vegetable oils | 1972 | 1·0 | 0·6 | 0·9 | 1·0 | 0·8 | 0·3 | 0·3 | 0·6 |
| Chemicals | 1960 | 4·9 | 4·5 | 7·2 | 6·6 | 3·9 | 3·1 | * | * |
|  | 1972 | 8·3 | 6·3 | 8·1 | 8·0 | 5·8 | 3·3 | 0·3 | 0·6 |
| Manufactured goods | 1960 | 16·7 | 23·7 | 16·6 | 23·1 | 16·7 | 23·3 | * | * |
| by material | 1972 | 21·1 | 22·4 | 15·8 | 20·1 | 20·8 | 18·9 | 9·1 | 12·0 |
| Machinery and | 1960 | 14·5 | 9·6 | 13·0 | 21·6 | 7·5 | 10·1 | * | * |
| transport | 1972 | 26·3 | 19·3 | 20·8 | 24·2 | 20·1 | 28·7 | 10·2 | 26·6 |
| Miscellaneous | 1960 | 2·5 | 6·6 | 2·9 | 5·6 | 3·7 | 6·7 | * | * |
|  | 1972 | 9·0 | 11·5 | 4·4 | 11·8 | 8·0 | 11·4 | 4·8 | 5·6 |
| Others | 1960 | 0·4 | 0·7 | 0·3 | 1·1 | 0·5 | 2·9 | * | * |
|  | 1972 | 0·1 | 2·8 | 0·5 | 1·0 | 1·2 | 3·1 | 0·7 | 0·1 |

**Exports by Commodities—1960/1972**
(percentage of total exports)

|  |  | France | G'many | Italy | Neth. | U.K. | U.S.A. | Japan | Spain |
|---|---|---|---|---|---|---|---|---|---|
| Foods and live | 1960 | 9·9 | 1·6 | 13·7 | 25·5 | 2·9 | 13·3 | * | * |
| animals | 1972 | 10·3 | 3·2 | 6·7 | 20·3 | 3·6 | 11·6 | 2·3 | 24·8 |
| Beverage and | 1960 | 3·3 | 0·3 | 1·7 | 1·1 | 2·7 | 2·4 | * | * |
| tobacco | 1972 | 3·5 | 0·3 | 2·1 | 1·2 | 3·2 | 1·9 | 0·1 | 4·5 |
| Crude | 1960 | 8·1 | 2·6 | 4·2 | 6·9 | 3·4 | 13·7 | * | * |
| materials | 1972 | 4·9 | 2·1 | 1·9 | 6·0 | 3·2 | 10·3 | 1·7 | 3·6 |
| Mineral | 1960 | 3·9 | 6·0 | 6·0 | 11·7 | 3·8 | 4·1 | * | * |
| fuel | 1972 | 2·3 | 2·6 | 4·4 | 12·0 | 2·4 | 3·2 | 0·3 | 4·4 |
| Animal and | 1960 | 0·3 | 0·3 | 0·2 | 1·3 | 0·2 | 1·5 | * | * |
| vegetable oils | 1972 | 0·4 | 0·4 | 0·2 | 1·0 | 0·1 | 1·0 | 0·1 | 2·7 |
| Chemicals | 1960 | 8·6 | 11·0 | 7·1 | 8·3 | 8·9 | 8·5 | * | * |
|  | 1972 | 9·5 | 11·7 | 6·6 | 13·6 | 9·9 | 8·5 | 6·2 | 5·5 |
| Manufactured goods | 1960 | 32·1 | 25·9 | 26·4 | 20·7 | 26·3 | 14·7 | * | * |
| by material | 1972 | 21·9 | 20·6 | 22·1 | 17·8 | 24·2 | 10·0 | 28·9 | 2·4 |
| Machinery and | 1960 | 24·7 | 43·4 | 27·7 | 18·7 | 43·1 | 34·3 | * | * |
| transport | 1972 | 33·5 | 48·3 | 35·6 | 20·6 | 41·2 | 43·8 | 47·8 | 30·2 |
| Miscellaneous | 1960 | 8·3 | 8·4 | 12·6 | 4·6 | 6·5 | 6·7 | * | * |
|  | 1972 | 9·8 | 9·3 | 20·0 | 7·5 | 9·5 | 6·5 | 11·9 | 21·8 |
| Others | 1960 | 1·0 | 0·5 | 0·4 | 1·1 | 2·4 | 1·1 | * | * |
|  | 1972 | 4·0 | 1·5 | 0·4 | 0·6 | 2·8 | 3·2 | 0·9 | 0·1 |

*Source:* OECD, *Trade by Commodities,* January–December 1972
*Data not available

# CHAPTER III

## SOME STARK TRUTHS FOR BRITAIN

The real economic condition of Britain, then, is one of diminishing competitiveness, deteriorating balance of payments and declining standards of living. Until very recently this economic and social decline had not been so marked. Britain had been growing, but more slowly than other countries. Yet in 1974, for the first time in the postwar era, Britain's individual wealth registered an absolute decline and it is almost certain that this relative retardation will shortly translate itself into a long-range absolute decline. Unless heroic efforts are made on a national scale there will be many such years—intermittent but frequent—an insidious and protracted process of loss of real national income and shrinking personal welfare. This is a perilous situation, and all the more so because Britain as a whole refuses to face the facts.

This bleak forecast is insistently rejected. The arguments against such a view of Britain's future—for the most part stereotyped arguments—thus deserve discussion in some detail. Yet before taking these up it may be useful to say a word about economic growth in general. The issue is a serious one for in spite of the real problems created by the oil crisis—rising unemployment, for example—and the energetic efforts of most governments today to stimulate growth and employment, it is still common in some circles to ask whether economic growth is desirable, or whether the costs of growth in terms of quality of life may not simply be too high. The brief answer is that in a period of general prosperity such as the advanced nations have experienced for the last two decades, it is easy to discount the material component of popular well-being, but surely it is clear too that the quality of life in a nation has fundamentally to do with whether the national economy provides the means to a decent livelihood for its citizens.

**Why economic growth**

If a country does not grow, and the national economy is uncompetitive in the international marketplace, and real wages based on real productivity do not keep up with the international inflation from which no major state is isolated, the outcome can be not simply economic crisis but political and social upheaval. It can be argued plausibly that Britain today is simply suffering the consequence of a long period in which its economic growth has lagged behind the growth of neighbouring, competing economies whose living standards are still compared to the British standard of life. The British miner today makes far less than the Belgian miner—and before the recent wage rises he made less than the Spanish miner. But the British standard of living is certainly not lower than the Spanish, nor does it seem that the British people are reconciled to seeing their living standards, their public services, or their influence as a nation, fall below the level of their truly prosperous European neighbours.

But is the problem then solely one of comparative performance? The larger debate questions the validity of economic expansion itself. There is popular disquiet today over the costs and implications of economic growth, though these are perhaps less marked since the oil crisis sent unemployment statistics soaring in the United Kingdom, the United States and West Germany.

Before we attempt a comment on the larger issues at stake, let us make some simple definitions and qualifications. Growth rates and the indices of GNP measure the flow of goods and services in a country. They are among the most useful measures of the vitality of a national economy, *but they are neither comprehensive nor precise.* They are not always comparable among nations and the value of such figures obviously varies according to the quality of the statistics that back them up and these are not the same for all countries. The value of an index of GNP *per capita* is even more variable as a measure of real individual well-being since the total wealth of countries obviously is distributed in vastly different ways even among the consumer societies of Western Europe. All are egalitarian, but some are more egalitarian than others. And *per capita* GNP comparisons between the Western industrial nations and those of the Eastern European socialist bloc are certainly very unreliable and often positively misleading unless they are given extensive qualification. Not only are value systems different, but the consumer sector in the socialist states of Europe is, as a matter of state policy, greatly retarded by comparison with the West. Indeed, the word "retarded" would no doubt be unacceptable to an Eastern European or Soviet or Chinese Communist commentator, who would reject that the consumer society is a proper form of social organisation at all.

Nonetheless we have used the tools that are available. The indices of GNP and GNP *per capita* tell us something we would not otherwise know in a tangible or numerical fashion. They allow us to make qualified comparisons between economies. When states are roughly parallel in economic organisation and assumptions, with conscientious national statistical agencies—as is the case with the Western European and North American industrial nations and Japan—the comparisons have real authority.

Are the things they tell us worth knowing? The answer seems clear: if you are interested in the commercial, industrial and economic performance and power of societies, and of societies in relation to one another, yes. These figures are indicators of vitality, even if they are not explanations or interpretations of that vitality.

On the other hand, GNP rates are not statements about human happiness or fulfilment. Life is made neither of bread alone nor of economic product. GNP rates can only indicate whether a great many people are eating well or eating badly in a society. But we are not so far from the Great Depression of the 1930s,

55

or so invulnerable to its repetition, that we can afford to redefine "quality of life" with too cavalier a disregard for its economic component.

## The limits of growth

The growth debate raises issues of resource exhaustion and environmental pollution. Both are valid concerns although they are distinct. Pollution, on the evidence of the modern industrial experience, is a more serious threat to the future, and a more serious objection to "unrestrained" growth, than the question of exhausting our resource reserves. An irreversible corruption of certain elements in our natural environment is perfectly possible. As a habitat for fish, no doubt the lower reaches of the River Tees are finished. Lake Baikal in the USSR and the Adriatic Sea may be dying. Certainly these are important, but the argument about resources, which dominated discussion in Europe a year or two ago seems to be almost over. The resources argument has been the victim of overexposure, overstatement, and the misinterpretation of our experience with resource use, and the recent energy crisis seems paradoxically to have killed it.* As a logical proposition it is true that since the earth's resources are finite and their consumption rises at an expanding rate, then they must ultimately be exhausted. The interesting question is: When? Our actual experience has often been that resources "expand" with use. Exploration and the improvement of techniques of extraction and refinement actually enlarge the pool of available resources—as, for example, we begin to explore the mineral resources under the seas. Moreover, the forms of resources have changed as the economy and technology have changed. Coal and hydroelectric power have succeeded wood as an energy source, oil has succeeded coal and nuclear and solar energy technologies are now beginning to make an appearance. It would be foolish for man to be indifferent to the problems of resource reserves, but the debate surrounding the Club of Rome † seems in retrospect curiously naive, as was that report's own use of data and its reliance upon a grandiose computer technique (Professor Forrester's "system dynamics" model) to demonstrate a simple thesis.

So far as resources go, the "zero growth" remedy to the problem of the world in general and Britain in particular also seems irrelevant, if only because it proposes an impossible solution. The Western world in the nineteenth and twentieth centuries has been dominated by two great reforming visions; first a popular sharing out of the wealth of society, and second a popular sharing out of political

---

*Published as D. H. Meadows, D. L. Meadows, J. Randers, and W. W. Behrens III, *The Limits of Growth* (London, 1972). A number of sytematic critiques of the methods as well as the assumptions of the study have since been published, among them a Hudson Institute (New York) paper, E. S. Boylan, *A Critical Analysis of Forester's "World Dynamics"*, HI-1632-DP (1972) and Wilfred Beckerman's more recent work *The Defence of Economic Growth* (London, 1974).

†It is noteworthy that in its October 1974 meeting in Berlin, the Club of Rome retracted its earlier gloomy predictions of the early exhaustion of the earth's natural resources as mathematically incorrect.

power. Both wealth and power were once controlled by a minority. Today, however imperfectly, and after much revolutionary bloodshed, wealth and power are more widely held. Political reform has produced economic change, and the chief mechanism by which wealth has been distributed to the common man has been through the creation of new industrial wealth. There has been some dispossession of the old holders of wealth, both among nations and among individuals. But if the wealth of the world as a whole or of any particular society were fixed, its complete redistribution would have only negligible benefits for the mass of nations and people. The argument for redistributing the wealth of the rich has been largely social and moral, not economic: in purely economic terms the effort would change little. Historically this has been true, and it remains largely true today, except that the really wealthy in today's world are whole nations of people.

The political implications of zero growth are therefore revolutionary—or counter-revolutionary. If wealth is fixed, then either the fixed quantity will be redistributed (and this is most unlikely to be a peaceful process even within nations and almost unimaginable as between the industrial nations and the Third World) or else the present inequalities of wealth will be maintained, and that implies national and international repression. The rich, including the rich nations, are also usually the effective possessors of the instruments of power. The implications of zero growth, taken seriously, are of a profound and enduring struggle between the possessors of wealth and the dispossessed, on a world-wide scale.

Of course no such implications were intended. The controversy has never really been intellectually serious. Faced with the dismay which even the current economic problems of the world have provoked one might ask what people thought zero growth would really be like. The answer is that the critics of growth in fact usually have been critics of the social order and of the aesthetics of growth. Such critics question the existing distribution of wealth, and recoil from the violence done to nature by industrialism. Distrusting the values of the consumer marketplace, the tastelessness of much urban and suburban housing, the triviality of much that is manufactured, the amorality of much advertising, they are profoundly disturbed by the impact urbanisation and industrialisation have had upon society and the community. Very often they have been open or secret conservatives, even élitists, defenders of established or traditional values threatened by the economic democracy of the consumer society. Sometimes, even without recognising their own motives, they have been defenders of privilege and those forms of status which are jeopardised by popular affluence. They have sometimes deserved the furious response of the Marxists, who say that zero growth is a ruling-class ideology determined to protect the upper class (including academics and the professional bourgeoisie as well as the traditional capitalist élites) at the cost of perpetual austerity for the working man and his family.

The debate over growth today is more often than not a reformulation of criticisms that have little to do with whether economies should grow. It seems to us clear that people in industrial societies like Britain are not really troubled today because they are too rich, or because they are unwilling to admit that they cannot go on indefinitely getting richer. They are troubled by certain social, emotional, and moral costs of a highly bureaucratised and technologically orientated society, and by the values of industrialism. In the British case, they are troubled by the conflict between the harsher realities of modern industrialism and a certain persistent English deream of countryside and rural innocence that has both an aristocratic and popular currency. Britons are not very often ambivalent about the utility of wealth itself. Every ordinary man understands that it is better to be well-housed, well-fed, decently shod, and healthy; and to possess the money for luxuries or trivialities, than to be poor. It is better to have a motorcycle than a bicycle for travelling to work, and it is better still to have a car, whatever the traffic. The wealth of Europe today clearly is thought by virtually every European, with sound reason, to be a good thing, an unmistakable benefit. The British are not signally different. The anxieties of Britain's urban and industrial society derive from quite different sources.

**The modern anxiety**

The zero growth argument can be called a disguised ideology of privilege, or a form of romantic reaction, or a utopianism expressed in the language of the computer. It is necessary to say these things, but it is also necessary to acknowledge that the argument expresses a persistent anxiety of a peculiarly modern kind. This anxiety might be interpreted as the secular formulation of the much older debate between materialism and a non-materialist value system. The simplest form of the question being asked is, 'Isn't there more to life than this?' The simple answer, of course, is 'Yes'. The question implies a recoiling not merely from the materialism of our society, or from the vulgarity and waste that are a part of contemporary industrialism and the consumer society, but a doubt about industrialism and technology themselves.

The industrial system has in two centuries brought about a profound change in human life and human consciousness. On the one hand it has brought the mass of men to an unprecedented level of economic well-being. On the other hand it has created instruments and systems of power, organisation, and manipulation that can be and have been indiscriminately turned to destructive and degrading use. "In no other civilisation has man been so totally repressed". That is an accusation made both by Herbert Marcuse, the neo-Marxist and neo-Freudian critic of the alleged suppression of libido and spontaneity in modern society and by the Christian sociologist and philosopher Jacques Ellul. Ellul, unlike Marcuse, is no enemy of structure, discipline and responsibility in society, nor—to adapt the arguments of Freud—does he doubt the creativity of libidinal sublimation. Ellul makes a different charge: that men are repressed because the industrial and technological organisation of society constitutes a 'social machine' whose dominating values are inhumane. Private life, the ultimate refuge of a humane culture, is diminished, and Ellul would argue that politics have been turned into a series of meaningless choices among alternate formulations of the same totalitatian ends. Political struggle and tension, he says, "empty into a void" because undamental choices have already been determined—not by evil leaders or conspiratorial groups, or by capitalism or socialism in themselves, but by the workings of the social machine itself. "Capitalism did not create our world; the machine did."*

In this perspective the question of economic growth merely touches upon one element in a technological society which steadily works to the aggrandisement of every aspect of its collective power. Ellul seems to us to make a far more penetrating analysis than the liberal critics of growth (or the contemporary Marxists—who in any event are no enemies of economic growth). What reply can be made to his assertion that Western society has become a value-free, totalitarian social machine, dominated by technique and the aggrandisement of power? It must simply be said that Britain, like the other Western European and North American industrial states, has made a certain historical choice, and irrevocable consequences have followed. Britain's industrialism is not to be undone. The age of technology derives directly and necessarily from the age of science and rationalism, Britain's noontime years.

Britain's possibilities today thus are not unlimited. The country can mitigate the consequences of industrialism and technology in society, make a more humane distribution of the material benefits of industry, and attempt to control the workings of the system with greater discrimination and intelligence. But Marx himself once observed that money is the principle of the inauthentic in a society. "Let us assume man to be man, and his relation to the world a human one. Then love can only be exchanged for love, trust for trust, etc. . . "† The concern he was articulating was common to the nineteenth century, as it is to the twentieth—that man may not be fully human anymore, and that his relation to the natural world is ceasing to be a humane one.

This is what the growth argument is really all about, and thus it represents an expression of an anxiety about the forces of modern society that has been part of modern consciousness for three centuries. Modern man is also divided man; the modern mind is divided—in tension. Again and again there are attempts to resolve the tension through a simple choice between land and machine, individual relationships and collective relationships; total (and implicitly totalitarian) materialism, and the rejection of the material world itself along with rationalism and technique. Each of these simple choices has failed. Yet this still does not seem to us a warrant for absolute pessimism.

To accept such pessimism is to deny that history continues to be process. It is to believe that we are at the terminal point of history. To concede pessimism is also

---

*Jacques Ellul, *The Presence of the Kingdom* (New York, 1967), p.77.
†Karl Marx, *Early Writings* (London, 1963), pp. 193-194.

to deny the modern inheritance itself, its intellectual energy and its Faustianism. It is to hold that we are in a trap, that morally and historically we are caged. It seems to us that the problem growth poses is a problem we already know all too well, but resist acknowledging. The importance of the Faustian myth in Western literature, and of the myths of Prometheus and of Pandora's fatal box, must not be underestimated. They express our consciousness of the power Western civilisation possesses, its ambition—and our knowledge that this power will too often be misused to destructive ends. Britain has been central to the history of the West. In Marlowe's Faustus and in Isambard Kingdom Brunel, the near-mythic "Great Engineer", we see the Promethean figure.

For what has always set Western (and British) civilisation apart from other cultures has been its exploitative attitude towards the material world. From the time of Jehovah's injunction to Adam to name the beasts and till the earth, and be master of all that is in and on the earth, ours has been a civilisation of material exploitation. Our relationship to the material world has always been coercive, violent. This has made us what we are. Our persistent anxiety over where our civilisation will lead us in the future is justified. The Western World and Britain no less, is historically a civilisation estranged from the "natural order", a technological civilisation. Other cultures have conformed to nature, have been passive before it, but Europeans have defied natural limits. Contrary to Marx, it is not mere money which is the principle of inauthenticity in modern society; western society in itself has always had an "inauthentic" relationship to the natural world and the natural order.

No doubt this seems to bring us a long way from GNP and the debate over growth. But the following point seems to us a crucial one: the West is a society which has always furiously expanded, making tools and machines, seeking practical knowledge and wealth. It was Britain which made the first leap into industrial modernity, leading the world. It might be better if it had not been this way. But it will do Britain no good to deny the nature of its society and culture, or look for sentimental resolutions of a problem which is at the very core of Western civilisation. Britain is a "growth society" by culture; it is also a Faustian society. Being what it is, it is rightfully apprehensive over the use it makes of technological power and the price it must pay for its civilisation. But conversely, Britain, in its wealth, has lain at the centre of the not inconsiderable Western humane civilisation as well.

**The specific British dimension**

Britain is a country of 56 million people living on a crowded and poor island, in no sense self-sufficient in food or raw materials and, as we have seen, decreasingly self-sufficient even in manufactured goods. There is no possibility of supporting Britain's population except through the mechanism of modern industrial society; the options of retreat into a rural, stable-state society or zero-growth economy are sentimentalities.* The result of such an effort would be widespread economic distress, and if the process were carried far enough, actual physical distress and finally hunger.

How unfavourable is Britain's position in respect to food as compared to the country's EEC partners is set forth in Table 13. Britain imports 42 per cent. of her wheat, 21.5 per cent of her beef, 30.9 per cent of her pork, and 84.97 per cent of her butter. In all, the nation imports about half its food at a current cost of well over £2,000 million†. One may estimate that even at severely reduced standards of diet Britain could at most support perhaps 40 million people. A statement like this one may seem trivial or self-evident and thus not worth making; but Britain's state is in fact so perilous, its postwar history so long a series of misfortunes and blasted hopes, that the nation as a whole has tended to generate extraordinarily tenacious illusions and myths, designed either to deny that the national decline is real or to suggest that, if real, it hardly matters at all. These defensive reactions cover a broad spectrum, from escape into the persistent fantasies of English country life, to naked assertions of the continuing supremacy of the English quality of life over that of others, to pure xenophobia—a xenophobia which asserts that whatever Britain's neighbours or the Americans may be doing in the world is simply irrelevant to Britain. In the following pages we shall therefore discuss certain stereotypical reactions—not least because they are likely to be raised upon the publication of this book.

The first and obvious reaction to arguments about Britain's decline is the assertion that the invidious comparisons between Britain and other countries are simply not true. The data are said to be misleading or false, or the doomsayers, for whatever reason, simply lie. Thus the idea of Britain's being on a par, in terms of *per capita* income, with Italy in the early 1980s is rejected out of hand. Futurology, it is said, is pretentious nonsense.

**Table 14.  Percentage Imports/Total Indigenous Consumption in 1971**

| Wheat | |
|---|---|
| UK | 42.44 |
| France | 2.96 |
| Germany | 34.72 |
| Italy | 14.18 |
| **Beef** | |
| UK | 21.5 |
| France | 6.5 |
| Germany | 13.48 |
| Italy (Beef & Veal) | 43.31 |

*In the middle of the 19th century the population of Ireland fell from 8 to less than 6 million, due to widespread starvation and mass emigration. This negative population trend began to reverse itself only in the decade of the 1950s, and it goes without saying that Ireland's demographic and economic decline was accompanied by much social and political tension and personal grief.

†*Agriculture's Import Saving Role,* HMSO (London, 1968), p.4.

|        | **Pork** |       |
|--------|:--------:|------:|
| UK     |          | 30.92 |
| France |          | 17.1  |
| Germany|          | 10.86 |
| Italy  |          | 21.28 |
|        | **Butter** |     |
| UK     |          | 84.97 |
| France |          | 0.4   |
| Germany|          | 8.44  |
| Italy  |          | 36.11 |

Source: OECD Food Consumption Statistics 1955-1971.

'Futurology', whatever the validity of this so-called new science, strikes us, too, as a pretentious term and an ugly one as well. Those who have collaborated on this report admit readily that speculation on the far future can only remain speculation, which may be more or less interesting according to the given case. What we are talking about in this book, however, is Britain today, tomorrow and the day after tomorrow. That is not futurology. One can make serious remarks about the near future for the simple reason that it is implicit in decisions, events, and tendencies discernible in the present. Unless certain major events take place—a total worldwide catastrophe, which would of course further darken the prospects, or a major national reversal of mood or attitude such as we would hope to see—then the results we have forecast for Britain in 1980 can hardly be evaded. Even if this report were to be followed by the kind of national reforms we might hope for, a significant turnaround in existing trends before the 1980s is highly unlikely. The existing facts and tendencies in the British situation are unmistakable. To claim that this is untrue or that their outcome cannot possibly be foreseen is to be like a man told by his doctor that he suffers a terminal disease insisting on a general discussion on whether prognosis is feasible at all.

Reality is difficult to grasp even if the facts and numbers are overwhelming. The good fortune of Britain over the past three or four centuries makes the sombre forecasts seem incredible. In the past, when things have seemed dark, Britain has still always pulled through. God, for centuries, has seemed to be an Englishman, but the truth is that no nation is exempt from the laws of growth and decay.

### The arguments in defence of the status quo

A second and frequent argument against Britain's decline is that while the forecasts for Britain may in general be valid, the national decline will nevertheless be mitigated by compensatory factors. It is said, for example, that the whole world is in economic decline, and that Britain's plight must thus be hardly noticeable in the general debacle. Or it is argued that 'We won't need the Concorde anyway', i.e. there is a simple solution in scrapping ambitious but unnecessary projects. Or it is said that 'England will always be England', and the special qualities of social and individual life in Britain will persist and will compensate for a decline calculated in purely material terms.

In our opinion the decline will be mitigated by nothing. Britain's present economic difficulties are in no sense part of a universal collapse due to an energy or raw materials shortage. The British decline has been evident for years (even though it may have emerged into public consciousness only this year). Nor is it true that since the outbreak of the oil crisis all growth elsewhere has stopped. As the following tables demonstrate, *for the greater part of the developed world growth has gone on since the Yom Kippur War*. It has merely been reduced in the various countries by an average of 1-2 per cent.

Arnold Toynbee to the contrary, the wealth of Western civilisation is not "melting away"*. France and Belgium, for example, have sustained fairly *high* rates of growth even since the Arab-Israeli war of 1973 and are quite likely to continue so. Even the Italian economy, it would appear, is in better condition than Britain's. The industrial productivity index is higher, and Italy will experience positive growth this year while Britain is virtually certain to register negative growth. Finally, it must be understood that if there were worldwide economic collapse on the model of 1929-32, Britain's condition would be still worse than that of her neighbours since the United Kingdom is one of the least self-sufficient economies in the world. What is at issue is Britain's ability to compete in world markets for increasingly dear (and sometimes scarce) raw materials and goods. It is well-known that commodity and raw material prices have been rapidly rising, and even though these prices will fluctuate the long-range forecast is for continued rise. Britain will be competing for these materials against other nations far richer and better able to buy them.

## Table 15
### EEC Industrial Production since October 1973
#### (1970=100)

| | 1973 | | | 1974 | | | | | |
|---|---|---|---|---|---|---|---|---|---|
| | Oct. | Nov. | Dec. | Jan. | Feb. | Mar. | Apr. | May | June |
| FRANCE | 122 | 123 | 119 | 125 | 126 | 123 | 124 | 126 | 127 |
| % I or D† | — | 0.82 | 3.35 | 5.04 | 0.80 | 2.38 | 0.81 | 1.61 | 0.79 |
| GERMANY | 115 | 116 | 116 | 114 | 117 | 114 | 114 | 114 | 118 |
| % I or D | — | 0.87 | 0.00 | 1.78 | 2.63 | 2.56 | 0.00 | 0.00 | 3.51 |
| ITALY | 118 | 117 | 117 | 124 | 119 | 120 | 124 | 122 | — |
| % I or D | — | 0.85 | 0.00 | 5.98 | 4.03 | 0.84 | 4.17 | 2.4 | — |
| UNITED KINGDOM | 113 | 111 | 107 | 100 | 104 | 107 | 109 | 110 | 109 |
| % I or D | — | 1.77 | 3.60 | 6.54 | 4.00 | 2.88 | 1.87 | 0.92 | 0.91 |
| BELGIUM | 116 | 121 | 115 | 128 | 126 | 121 | 126 | 128 | — |
| % I or D | — | 4.31 | 4.96 | 11.30 | 1.56 | 3.97 | 4.13 | 1.59 | — |
| LUXEMBOURG | 116 | 126 | 117 | 125 | 128 | 121 | 118 | 117 | 121 |
| % I or D | — | 8.62 | 7.14 | 6.83 | 2.4 | 5.47 | 2.48 | 0.85 | 3.42 |
| NETHERLANDS | 130 | 129 | 128 | 130 | 131 | 131 | 130 | 131 | 132 |
| % I or D | — | 0.77 | 0.77 | 1.56 | 0.77 | 0.00 | 0.76 | 0.77 | 0.76 |
| TOTAL EEC | 117 | 118 | 116 | 117 | 118 | 117 | 118 | 118 | 121 |
| % I or D | — | 0.85 | 1.69 | 0.86 | 0.85 | 0.85 | 0.85 | 0.00 | 2.54 |

†Increase or Decrease
*Source:* Main Economic Indicators, OECD, Sept. 1974.

*The Observer* (London) September 8, 1974

## Table 16
## Growth of Real GDP in Selected European Countries
(Percentage changes seasonally adjusted from previous half-year)

### Estimates and Forecasts

| | 1973 | | 1974 | | 1975 |
|---|---|---|---|---|---|
| | I | II | I | II | I |
| FRANCE (GDP) | 6.6 | 5.5 | 4.75 | 4.5 | 4.25 |
| GERMANY | 9.1 | 0.3 | 2 | 3.5 | 4.25 |
| ITALY | 4.2 | 9.8 | 2.5 | 0 | 1.5 |
| UK (GDP) | 8.4 | 0.4 | – 6 | 4.5 | 1.25 |

*Source:* OECD, Economic Outlook, July 1974.

This is bad enough. But based upon a sense of itself as a prosperous society, an advanced society, Britain's wants and necessities are those of Britain's wealthier neighbours. Nor are all of these perceived needs frivolous; they include advanced medical equipment, kidney machines, for example. Even if world inflation is brought down from its present disastrous levels, the long-range trend remains inflationary, and *Britain will more and more have to replace its current infrastructure at increasingly high prices on the world market.* Britain, in a few years, may not be able to afford not only supersonic airplanes, but essential social services—health, education, old age insurance among them—even at present inadequate levels. Initially only relatively peripheral areas will be touched; but eventually the poverty of services will cut close to the bone. In the case of Britain's inability to afford, say, advanced diagnostic equipment, which her neighbours can afford, the inability will seem brutal. Just as underdeveloped countries cannot afford such things now, Britain, given its present performance, may well not be able to afford them in the 1980s. And the problem will not be seriously alleviated by a simple redistribution of wealth, when the total wealth is itself in absolute decline.

### "The British Way of Life"

Next, there are those in Britain who think that national economic decline will be mitigated or compensated for by maintenance of the "British way of life"—in effect the country's peculiar traditions. As a multinational group who visit the country often, the authors certainly would not deny the attractive features of what is commonly thought of as the British life-style. But we would note also that these seem more often than not to be the prerogative of the privileged classes—and the privileged areas—of the United Kingdom. While no one can seriously doubt that Britain is a political democracy, it is certainly a class-ridden democracy*. The British may reproach foreigners, particularly

---

*It is also entirely insular to assume that Britain is significantly more democratic than a half-dozen other advanced societies of Western Europe. It is arguably a more successful and complete democracy than postwar France or Italy, but hardly significantly more democratic than Western Germany (since the war) and certainly no more democratic in any respect than Denmark, the Netherlands, Sweden or Norway. It would be hard to make the argument, for example, that civil liberties are better protected in Britain than in Scandinavia.

64

Americans, for their "obsession" with the class features of British life, but even to the best disposed foreigner these denials seem quite unsustainable. If it is true that since the time of the first postwar Labour government a social "revolution" has occurred, it has not brought an end to class privilege and ensured egalitarian distribution of wealth. As Table 17 shows, one per cent of Britain's population in 1971 still owned 20.4 per cent of the wealth; 2 per cent owned 27 per cent. More striking is that the top 50 per cent owned 90.2 per cent of the wealth, which is to say that the disfavoured 50 per cent of the population altogether owned only 9.8 per cent. This is hardly an egalitarian distribution of wealth, even granting improvements over the last decade. In comparative terms it is hardly better than the Italian pattern and much less favourable than the Swedish. Moreover, Britain appears, compared to most of its continental neighbours, to be a society in which those who possess the wealth are not in-

### Table 17. Wealth of Individuals in Great Britain

|  |  | 1961 | 1965 | 1966 | 1970 | 1971 |
|---|---|---|---|---|---|---|
| Distribution of wealth by groups of owners | | | | | | |
| Percentage of wealth owned by: | | | | | | |
| Most wealthy 1 per cent | | 28.4 | 24.4 | 23.6 | 20.7 | 20.4 |
| „ „ 2 „ „ | | 37.1 | 32.7 | 31.0 | 28.0 | 27.7 |
| „ „ 3 „ „ | | 42.7 | 38.4 | 35.9 | 33.0 | 32.8 |
| „ „ 4 „ „ | | 47.0 | 42.8 | 40.2 | 37.0 | 36.8 |
| „ „ 5 „ „ | | 50.6 | 46.4 | 43.7 | 40.9 | 40.1 |
| „ „ 10 „ „ | | 62.5 | 58.6 | 56.0 | 51.9 | 51.6 |
| „ „ 25 „ „ | | 79.2 | 77.7 | 75.1 | 72.5 | 72.1 |
| „ „ 50 „ „ | | 92.5 | 92.5 | 90.9 | 90.2 | 90.2 |
| All owners | | 100.0 | 100.0 | 100.0 | 100.0 | 100.0 |
| Total wealth (thousand million) | | 54.9 | 74.3 | 76.8 | 96.8 | 112.7 |

Source: Social Trends IV, HMSO (London) 1973.

hibited in its display.* We insist on this point—more or less self-evident to outsiders—because some features of the "British way of life", far from compensating for Britain's shrinking national wealth, may well become an increasingly intolerable aggravation.

It is difficult to make valid international comparisons of the distribution of wealth within countries because the statistics that are available for each country tend not to be equivalent. The following table derives from a series of inquiries made at the end of the 1960s by the *Readers' Digest* organisation, and it permits some rough comparisons. It indicates that the British distribution of wealth and that of France are approximately equivalent—which does not flatter Britain, since France notoriously is one of the least egalitarian of the advanced European

---

*Even in a country like France, which we would not choose as a model of wealth distribution, it is notable that excepting the Citroen SM, a high-performance sports coupé comparable perhaps to the Aston-Martin, the largest automobile produced and the usual choice of—bankers and prosperous businessmen—is the Citroen DS, a fairly ordinary-sized car. There is nothing in Paris remotely like the proliferation of Bentleys, Rolls-Royces and Daimlers in London's West End.

countries in its income and wealth distribution. Moreover, if the British think that the wealth patterns in their society resemble those of Scandanavia, the Netherlands or perhaps West Germany, the figures suggest the contrary.

**Table 18. Distribution of Family Income**

Percentage of adults living in families where net weekly income is:

| | Less than $47 | Between $48 and $143 | Over $144 |
|---|---|---|---|
| United Kingdom | 51% | 46% | 3% |
| West Germany | 29% | 68% | 3% |
| Netherlands | 34% | 61% | 5% |
| Sweden | 18% | 72% | 10% |
| Norway | 16% | 75% | 9% |
| France | 50% | 45% | 5% |

*Source:* Radioscopie de l'Europe, 1970.

Much talk about the British way of life represents little more than a simple chauvinist assertion of national identity. There is no doubt that the vast majority of Britons prefer to live in Britain and would prefer roast pork and apple sauce on Sunday to *perdreaux aux choux*. They are satisfied with their own national pattern of life, and they would certainly rather live as Britons than say, Spaniards, rich or otherwise. We do not doubt that this is true; but neither is it a particularly telling point to make, since no doubt most Spaniards would rather live as Spaniards than as Englishmen. Thus such statements say little about the actual quality of life from country to country.

The quality of life in any country would seem objectively to resolve itself into certain quantifiables, such as the availability of housing and housing space, central heating, running water, accessibility of place of work to home, safety in the streets, longevity, infant mortality, or the availability of education. By the standards of most developed nations, Britain ranks fairly high in, for example, living space *per capita,* but as we have shown in Chapter II, the comparisons with most other West European countries in terms of education, infant mortality, life expectancy, and certain other variables are not favourable.

The very kindliness, or lack of aggression, which characterises British social relations may not be entirely unconnected with the country's poor economic performance. If, as is certainly the case, it produces a relaxed environment and figures as one of the characteristics of British society most attractive to foreigners, it is doubtful if this advantage is sufficient to counterbalance the negative consequences. If economic decline continues, one may well ask whether very much will be left of Britain's civility, since one of the features already associated with this economic decline is a new militancy itself a reflection of the deterioration of social relations between the working classes and the middle and upper classes. There are increasing signs in Britain, not all of them attributable to IRA fanatics, of a willingness to resort to violence. The fact that bombs explode in London today may not be entirely unrelated to economics as well as politics.

Nor are the issues of economic decline on the one hand and the recent upsurge of nationalist feeling in Ulster, Scotland and Wales unrelated. Present-day separatist feeling in Scotland and Wales may foreshadow graver troubles—just as the miners' strike and the paralysis of the British economy in the winter of 1973-74 can be seen as a foretaste of other troubles that may come in the future. The point has been often made by historians that a policy in its growth phase does not usually expand solely by force of arms. A successful imperial role—or even one of paramouncy within a confederation—demands a cultural and economic vigour. An external image of competence and dynamism are needed so that at least the subordinated accord a grudging respect to the dominant power. It is evident, for example, that the handful of troops that Britain miantained in India in the 18th and 19th centuries would never have sufficed to control the sub-continent had it not been in part for the immense prestige of Britain and her civilisation. (The Sepoy Rebellion was, after all, put down largely with Indian troops, who willingly gave their loyalty to the British Raj). Britain is a United Kingdom, comprising at least four, possibly more, specific nationalities, of which the dominant one has, of course, always been the English. Decisions have always been made in Whitehall, whatever the political fictions might have been. The English have dominated the economy and have set the tone for the society at large. They succeeded as much by example and the respect they engendered in incorporating the most vigorous members of the national minorities into their own society.

But if the English are seen to fail, the sight cannot help but cause repressed resentments against an English hegemony to surface. For the national minorities, if they have respected England, have not always loved her. Thus one should understand that poor economic performance in Britain is not limited to economics in its ultimate effects. A process of economic decline may well end in the break-up of the United Kingdom. These remarks are, if one likes, an exercise in futurology: we are not suggesting that the break-up is near. But it seems to us that if present tendencies persist, by the late 1980s or 1990s, such a break-up may have become virtually inevitable.

**Rationalising decline**

Finally it is sometimes said that economic decline may prove a blessing in dis-guise by enabling Britons to get back to a better ordering of priorities. It is an irony that this attitude is exactly parallel to the attitude of the French in the early 19th century, after their defeat and humiliation at Waterloo. France saw its great rival Britain forging ahead with the Industrial Revolution and becoming the great industrial power that France then could not be.* David Landes has described this attitude in his distinguished history of industrialism in Europe:

> The France of Louis XIV and then again of Napoleon had dominated Europe, awed the rest of the world by her pomp and circumstance,

---

*Nineteenth-century technology was largely based on coal—which Britain had and France did not.

scintillated by her artistic and intellectual achievements. She had developed in the process, especially at the upper levels of society, a highly integrated set of values, suffused with a sense of satisfaction and superiority. As is characteristic in such cases of identification between way of life and values on the one hand and self-esteem on the other, her reaction to those areas of activity in which she could not achieve pre-eminence was simply to reject them as unworthy. Britain was more successful commercially? What else could one expect from a nation of shopkeepers?

The successive military and naval defeats by Britain, from Blenheim and Ramillies through Plassey and Quebec to Trafalgar and Waterloo, did not shake this conviction of superior virtue. On the contrary, they reinforced Britain's position as France's traditional rival and enemy and confirmed the French in their hostility to what was viewed as a competitive way of life. Especially after 1815 there was a tendency—alongside a powerful current of cultural and intellectual Anglophilia—to seek comfort for defeat by noting the evils that industrialism had brought to England: the periodic crisis, the hordes of blanched children slaving in the mills, the excrescent slums. Along with this went a tacit surrender of economic aspirations: France would never be able to compete with Britain in an industrial world based on coal and iron; hence the need for high protection and even prohibition to preserve a different kind of economy —a more humane economy based on family units of enterprise, a market place free of cannibalistic competition, a healthful balance between agriculture and industry. The consequences of this rejection of the new industrial civilisation for both public policy and entrepreneurial behaviour are not easy to measure if only because this factor blends in with many others. It was nevertheless extremely important in fixing dispositions and justifying them; for it was this value judgment that furnished the moral sanction for economic retardation.*

Such, it seems to us is the present state of mind in Britain—a state of mind found among intellectuals and working men and women alike.

The parallel can be continued. Along with this tendency of the French to congratulate themselves on the preservation of a humane society there was no equivalent will to adjust and reduce the nation's aspirations. French political and social ambitions remained great, even though the country's economic base was in process of erosion. The end of illusion came in 1870. France collided with a Prussia whose pretentions were in keeping with its infrastructure. The result was, of course, humiliating defeat for France and the beginning of a long series of misfortunes, which have only begun to reverse themselves since 1945.

Britain today does show itself willing to adjust foreign policy to the reality of a shrunken economy, but the real analogy with the French case is that social

---

*David Landes, *The Unbound Prometheus* (Cambridge, Mass. 1972) p. 551.

expectations in Britain have not been reduced in pace with the shrunken economic reality. As France was unwilling to reduce its political, military and diplomatic pretentions, so Britain today shows little sign of willingness to accept the austerity and lower living standards that poor economic performance demands.

The incompatability of expectations and capabilities may thus grow, and the result is all too likely to be tragedy. Neither the British working man nor the British manager seems very willing to adopt a lifestyle of austerity and self-denial. Certainly the sight of the ordinary Briton shopping on High Street at Christmas time gives little evidence of a national will to reduce consumption to pre industrial or early industrial levels.

The ultimate answer that must be given to those who say that economic decline does not matter, or that growth is too costly in its effect upon the environment, is to observe what decline already means in too many parts of Britain today. Not only is the physical environment polluted; but humanity is degraded. The real pollution is that which is caused by poverty and archaic industries. Teesside, or the worst industrial valleys of South Wales, are today not so distant from the scene described in the following passage from Dickens:

> It was a town of red brick, or of brick that would have been red if the smoke and ashes had allowed it; but as matters stood it was a town of unnatural red and black like the painted face of a savage. It was a town of machinery and tall chimneys, out of which interminable serpents of smoke trailed themselves for ever and ever, and never got uncoiled. It had a black canal in it, and a river that ran purple with ill-smelling dye, and vast piles of building full of windows where there was a rattling and a trembling all day long, and where the piston of the steam-engine worked monotonously up and down like the head of an elephant in a state of melancholy madness.
>
> It contained several large streets all very like one another, and many small streets still more like one another, inhabited by people equally like one another, who all went in and out at the same hours, with work, and to whom every day was the same as yesterday and tomorrow, and every year the counterpart of the last and the next.*

---

*Charles Dickens, *Hard Times*, Penguin (London 1970).

# CHAPTER IV

## THE MYTHS OF SALVATION

How does Britain get out of its troubles? What we have already said should make it clear that the web of circumstance in which the country is caught is only partly a matter of economic inefficiency, low productivity, and lack of competitiveness. These in turn derive from aspects of modern British culture and from certain British social institutions which have not fully accommodated themselves to the contemporary world. No doubt there is much in the contemporary world which hardly bears emulating; but that world cannot be ignored if the British people expect to function in it and make their living as an industrial nation.

But it is easier to ignore than to adapt, and there have been a series of major evasions of reality to characterise the British debate in recent years. These have made it easier for the country to avoid confronting what is wrong within the society and what might be done, within British society, to put it right. These evasions take the form of external solutions to what really is an internal problem, for example, by national membership in a larger international group which is efficient and prosperous. And now there is a new evasion, North Sea oil, which is supposed to render Britain prosperous without anyone being compelled to change what he does or the way in which he has always done it.

North Sea oil is probably the only one of these evasions, these myths of salvation, which deserves detailed analysis. Oil obviously will make a big difference to the country's energy situation and the balance of payments. We will make that analysis below, but first two other major contemporary evasions need cursory identification.

### Europe

The first of these is that membership in the European Economic Community can cure the British sickness. Perhaps few can quite believe the argument today, but only a few years ago, when Britain sought entry into the Community, the economic case that was made for membership was not held a foolish one. The simple argument was that competition within the EEC customs-free area for a proper share of the very large nine-nation market would compel British industry either to be efficient or to go bankrupt as it lost even its own formerly protected domestic market to fresh foreign competition.

In the event, developments have not taken place on anything like the required scale. The shock was not big enough to make a real difference. The complexity of Britain's situation resisted so simple and direct a solution. British producers had already been trading in Europe and the Europeans in the United Kingdom. Levelling the barriers that formerly existed made a difference, but not enough of a difference to accomplish fundamental reform in Britain. It was over-optimistic to have expected that it would. The European community is a trade area, not a clinic for sick economies or a course in economic electro-shock therapy. Undoubtedly being in Europe is good for the British economy and the long-term effects will be positive, assuming that Britain remains a member. Competition will have a long-term effect upon the level of efficiency in the UK, although it does not necessarily follow from this that it will do more than drive out the least efficient British companies and put European competitors in their place. Nothing in EEC membership will make an inefficient producer efficient if the reasons for his inefficiency go deeper than mere incompetent management. It may simply kill him off.

At the same time it must be said that the apparent future of the EEC is less glamorous than many of its enthusiasts have believed. It is quite possible that the Community has already attained roughly the best that it can accomplish; it is a successful customs union, an advantageously large trading area for its energetic members. The benefits are largely commercial, offering economies of scale, rationalisation, and efficiency to producers and traders. It is possible that further steps in economic co-operation will be taken, co-ordinating national policies on currency and in matters of social and trade legislation, and possibly even in military purchases or certain other very large-scale technological enterprises of obvious common interest. It is also quite possible that nothing very much more will be done. The present arrangements, on the whole, work well—arguments over the Common Agricultural Policy notwithstanding.

What is exceedingly unlikely is that Europe will become a political entity in any sense that involves major institutional change or the further serious grant of sovereignty. The big political change in Europe since the war has already happened. Western Europe, under the pressure of external forces, has changed from a collection of autonomous nations with warring interests into a grouping whose common political, security, and economic interests manifestly outweigh their internal differences. The change in global scale which has taken place with the rise of the United States and the USSR to "superpower" status has made manifest the cultural and even political homogeneity of Western Europe. "Europe" possesses a real community of interests as well as an identifiable, and felt, culture in common. This change, which is a big change in world politics, did not require the institutions of the EEC; those institutions merely ratified and consolidated a change that had already taken place. Britain inevitably is a member, on qualified terms, of this European community, whether it belongs to the EEC or not. It *is* merely a qualified member, a limited member, for historical and cultural reasons which persistently cause it to look somewhat uneasily towards Europe, and to look at the same time outward towards the sea; to feel itself different, and want to be different, not wholly European.

Thus the British people remain decidedly ambivalent about the EEC. It is possible that the United Kingdom may yet leave the European Community. If it does, it undoubtedly will be Britain which suffers the most. The Community

71

can live without Britain, while for Britain to leave after having been a member would, one fears, represent a real retreat into national isolation and unwarranted notions of national superiority. This would not only be a political retreat, but in some sense a moral retreat.

## The Atlantic alternative

One reason why Britain has always felt that it could be separate from Europe is because there is another community to which Britain belongs by language and institutions, and by a Protestant culture quite distinct from the predominantly Latin and Catholic character of Europe today. This community, which was once made up of the Commonwealth plus the United States, now has narrowed —in political terms—to the transatlantic tie with the United States. There still is a sense in Britain, wistful as the references today may be, of the reality and security of the "special relationship."

Historically, the special relationship was the product of the Second World War and it existed among a particular generation of Americans and Britons. It does not exist today. For the United States, it ended with the passing of the administration of Dwight Eisenhower and perhaps it ended even before, at Suez. President Kennedy had a real sympathy for the United Kingdom and many British friendships and ties, but it was his administration which deliberately subordinated the American link with Britain to an American interest in the evolution of an allied European Community. During the Kennedy years and into our own day, the real "special relationships" that have existed for the United States in its dealings with Western Europe have been, first, the relationship of hostility and competition with France, and next the relationship with Western Germany, from which the United States obtained significant military and economic support. The United Kingdom, meanwhile, was politically complacent, and militarily and economically of secondary importance in American calculations.

The Kennedy administration quite deliberately terminated the autonomous British nuclear deterrent through its Skybolt decision. With Britain then dependent upon American nuclear submarine and underwater missile technology, the American interest in controlling the nuclear arms of the non-Communist world was secured, with only France the incorrigible exception. This interest was articulated as an altruistic interest; and to a degree this was sincere, although the power motivation was more important than Americans themselves have ever been readily prepared to admit. Since the late 1950s, to American policymakers in the Pentagon and at the State Department, Europe has meant the EEC; the problem of Europe for Americans has been whether it would remain an allied Europe, maintaining an essentially dependent relationship with the United States which had prevailed since 1945, or whether it would become a "Gaullist" Europe. In this situation, the role of Britain was, in Washington's eyes, to influence Europe to keep the old relationship. The United States wanted

Britain to join the EEC to counterbalance France. If British policy had been anything except complacent, Washington would have opposed British membership in the EEC.

Lyndon Johnson was happy to have Harold Wilson tacitly support him in his conduct of the Vietnam War. Exactly because of the real cultural ties, Britain in those years was the only country whose disapproval could have had a seriously inhibiting effect upon American policy. Richard Nixon was also grateful to have Heath remain conspicuously silent when America bombed Hanoi over Christmas 1972. What did this British loyalty earn for Britain? Support for the pound sterling is the only response ordinarily offered, and support for sterling was in fact support for the dollar, and in the end, both were devalued. Certainly the United States made no reciprocal concessions to British feelings or advice in the general conduct of its policy. Johnson—as subsequent accounts have made plain—felt nothing but astonished and blasphemous impatience when Wilson took it upon himself to try to mediate the Vietnam War. The British initiatives were, to the United States government, impertinent irrelevancies.

The British should understand that there is little historical affection for Britain in the United States. Before World War II, there was very considerable popular hostility towards Britain, and the British Empire. This was in part a consequence of the very large German and Irish immigrant groups in the United States but also derived from the fact that Britain was the historical enemy of the United States, something rather easier to forget in London than in Washington. For Americans, there are ingrained memories of the War of Independence (when only the French saved the United States), the War of 1812 when the British burned the American capital, and the American Civil War when British sympathies and help went to the rebel Confederacy. The First World War was rather widely regarded in the United States, during the 1920s and 1930s, as an affair in which the United States had been ensnared by British duplicity and propaganda. The modern American regard for Britain is very much a product of Britain's lonely stand against the Nazis. And even then, the Second World War, for Americans, had as one of its secondary objectives the ending of old empires, the British Empire specifically included, as Winston Churchill bitterly recognised.

The Americans for whom the wartime alliance and common enterprise with Britain in fighting Nazi Germany provided the great adventure of their lives, are mostly gone from power now. Their successors feel a regard for Britain; they are conscious of the language and culture that is shared across the Atlantic; but their sympathies do not extend to making political and economic concessions to Britain that are not motivated by a direct American interest.

This may appear harsh but so many of the words spoken on such occasions as Pilgrim Society Dinners, and so many of the undeniable factors of cultural relationships between the two nations, are given a political significance that in the contemporary world they do not merit. The United States and Britain are friendly and culturally related nations; they are perhaps closer to one another than any other two major countries in the contemporary world. But this association is not one that offers Britain an identifiable and valid alternative to its Common Market membership, nor does the American association offer Britain the slightest economic advantage that is not open to any other nation enjoying most-favoured-nation trading relations with the United States (which, if the present American administration has its way, will include the Soviet Union). Britain should not confuse its own debate, on its own problems, with any notion that the Atlantic tie somehow offers a way out.

## North Sea oil

The growing British despondency of recent years has found one remedy in the mounting popular conviction that a new Eldorado was being mapped out beneath the North Sea waves. Increasing discoveries of natural gas were, in the 1960s, followed by major strikes of high-quality oil. The press and political circles began absorbing the technological vocabulary of energy production as the decade drew to a close. The pendulum years, to borrow an apt title of a book summarising the social and political characteristics of the 1960s, had ended on a note of vague hope.

As the dimensions of Britain's economic crisis grew broader over the early 1970s, notwithstanding the heady, but shortlived, "rush to growth" during 1972, the darkening shadows of Britain's prospects were steadily countered by greater and greater insistence that, thanks to the grace of North Sea oil, all would indeed be well. It was a sentiment that even, in its more extreme guise, captured the leader columns of *The Times* in the form of a simple exhortation to the nation to hang on until 1977, when this miracle of black gold would commence its works.

As the months went by the myth of North Sea oil refined itself into three particular illusions. First, the North Sea oil reserves, which grew in extent almost by the week, were represented as a guarantee of unlimited supplies of cheap oil that would make Britain independent of imports by 1980. This belief in cheap and abundant fuel was only further exaggerated by the four-fold increase in petroleum prices that followed the outbreak of war in the Middle East in October of 1973. The second illusion is that development of the North Sea fields would have a major effect on British industry. The third is that current payments deficits could and should be charged against anticipated future oil earnings.

There is little doubt that oil supplies from the British sector of the North Sea will all but eliminate the need for oil imports before 1985; the bulk of British import requirements will be wiped out before the end of this decade. Rough estimates of future British demand and local North Sea supply are outlined in the table. As can be seen there is even the likelihood of a small exportable surplus.

Table 16

**British Oil: Demand and Local Supply 1975-85**

(millions of barrels per year)

| | Demand* | Supply Optimistic | Pessimistic |
|---|---|---|---|
| 1975 | 750 | 36 | 36 |
| 1980 | 950 | 1000 | 840 |
| 1985 | 1200 | 1800 | 840 |

*Estimate.

*Source: Production and Reserves of Oil and Gas in the United Kingdom,* Department of Energy, HMSO, London 1974.

The danger lies in the fact that North Sea oil is, by world standards, extremely expensive. For the moment the high oil price that emerged during the winter of 1973-74 has obscured that fact but, as we shall demonstrate below, it is highly probable that world oil prices will show a modest fall towards the end of this decade, leaving Britain with plentiful supplies of an over-priced resource, to the detriment of her industry and living standards.

To begin with, the exploration and development costs of oil in the North Sea are considerably above those faced, say, in the Persian Gulf. The 1974 cost of ensuring a daily flow of one barrel, for example, is above £2000 in terms of drilling and further infrastructure. In other words, a North Sea well giving a daily supply of, say, 50,000 barrels, currently costs in excess of £10 million to sink. And such a well would provide for only about 2 per cent of Britain's total needs.

These production costs are, in any case, rising quite sharply, particularly as deeper and more hostile stretches of the continental shelf are brought within the exploration area. In addition one needs to include the financial costs of such exploration—the costs arising from the capital borrowing associated with such large-scale operations. As a result, it is possible that the final costs of production of a barrel of North Sea oil will be somewhere between $4 and $6. In the Persian Gulf a typical production cost is perhaps 30 or 40 cents.

This means that with a world price level for oil of around $11, the level reached after last year's increases, there is a margin of profit on North Sea production from which company needs and government tax levies can be met. But, at least for North Sea oil, this margin is quite small, and any future reductions in world oil prices could create serious pressures on the actual economics of production, exploration and distribution for Britain's new indigenous energy supplies.

**Lower oil prices?**

However, outside of a very few specialised quarters, the idea that world crude oil prices could ever fall is simply not considered as a serious possibility. In part this results from a generalised conviction that in the 1970s world of rampant inflation no price actually comes down. In part it is due to a popular belief that world resources are under the pressures of scarcity without discrimination; that we are literally running out of petroleum, and higher prices will accompany this process. And, clearly, there is the lingering fear that some external consideration, like world price movements, could suddenly cast doubt on the viability of this vast project now so widely regarded as a substitute for national effort. So the possibility of such a development is excluded.

It is our belief that there will, indeed, be an eventual decrease in the price levels of world crude oil by the end of this decade if the effects of inflation are discounted. The decrease will not be dramatic, but it could be sufficient to place strain on the margins of return by then operational for North Sea production. The principal cause of such a fall would be, in our view, the direct consequence of a continuing modest surplus of world oil supply over requirements. This, together with a slight increase in competitiveness between producers that could emerge by 1980 because of the growing geographic dispersal of production and the partial fragmentation of producer cartels, could lead to reductions in world oil prices of the order of $2 per barrel at today's prices.

A possible global supply/demand configuration for oil is set out in Table 17. As can be seen, under assumption (i) based on reductions in output for all areas and a continuation in Middle East production at rates common during the 1960s, there would be a surplus in the non-communist world of between 10 and 12 million barrels a day. In other words, there would be an over-supply equal to about four North Seas. But that is an unlikely prospect, although marginally feasible. A more realistic scenario, that represented by assumption (ii) in the table, is based on general falls in oil production world-wide, including a halving in the rate of growth of Middle East output over traditional levels. The result is adequacy, or even a small surplus, in crude oil supply in 1980.

Neither alternative takes into account the possibility of expanded Soviet production. Certainly, given greater Western technical assistance for exploitation of Soviet reserves, exports of some 10 million barrels a day from the Soviet Union by the end of the 1970s are possible, though, in the context of current Soviet energy policy, little more than that. There could, too, be a rapid increase in production and export of crude oil from the People's Republic of China, and other Far Eastern sources. Neither have we made allowance for conservation measures or the substitution of alternative energy sources that public policy in many developed economies will have promoted by that time.

In short, the outlook for world oil prices is one of growing downward pressures leading to a flattening or small drop in the five or six years to come. And the further prices drop, the greater becomes the danger that British investment plans linked to North Sea oil, and indeed the whole panoply of hopes that has been pinned to this bonanza off the coasts, will emerge as expensive daydreams.

76

Table 17.

## Too Much Energy in 1980?

(energy demand and supply, in millions of barrels per day oil equivalent)

|  | World* | US | W. Europe |
|---|---|---|---|
| Demand |  |  |  |
| 1973 | 87 | 37 | 24 |
| % growth | 4.7 | 3.5 | 4.5 |
| 1980 | 120 | 47 | 33 |
| Local supply (i) |  |  |  |
| 1973 | 88 | 32 | 9 |
| % growth | 6.0 | 3.0 | 6.0 |
| 1980 | 132 | 40 | 13.5 |
| Local supply (ii) |  |  |  |
| 1973 | 88 |  |  |
| % growth | 4.6 |  |  |
| 1980 | 121 |  |  |

*Non-communist world. (i) and (ii), see text for different hypotheses. "% growth" is annual average percentage growth assumed under these hypotheses. *Source:* International Petroleum Institute, with Hudson Europe estimates/hypotheses.

## Oil and industry

The second North Sea illusion is based on the conviction that the availability of such plentiful supplies of energy will allow for the revolutionary transformation of the structure and competitiveness of British industry.

In straightforward economic terms, the exploration, exploitation and eventual production of oil reserves on the scale represented by the North Sea fields should indeed provide a technological and investment fillip to the more dynamic sectors of British industry. Estimates of the actual size of the "offshore market"—the machinery and other equipment called for by offshore oil operations—differ, but few challenge the fact that this market will be immense in financial and technical breadth. Although estimates vary, and indeed increase with the passage of time and the inflation of costs, it is possible that North Sea developments could call for an *annual* spending of some $1500 million. This would break down in a typical year to around 35 per cent for drilling equipment, 30 per cent for platforms, 25 per cent for pipelines and 10 per cent for production processing.

The enormous capital expenditure and the demand for complex technology in this size of operation should, in theory, have a marked effect on a very large sector of British industry and finance. The increase in goods and services necessary for the continued development of the oil reserves, for production platforms, supply bases, drilling rigs, storage tanks, even the services related to oil production and refining, should provide heavy input into British industry

77

which would have a multiplier effect on other parts of the economy leading to considerable expansion in national output.

That, at least, is the theory. Yet, despite the enormous demands on heavy marine engineering and oil-related industries, the record of British industry in the first ten years of North Sea operations has been pitiful. The story is one of missed opportunities by British industry and government, and complacency on the part of the London financial community. As a result, the chance for industrial re-invigoration offered by North Sea developments is likely to prove one of the major economic myths of contemporary economic life.

There was, for example, no real provision made for the training of technical personnel for exploration work, on the lines of the Norwegian School of Navigation and Engineering. By the peak period of drilling operations around 1973-74, over 60 per cent of the drillers working the North Sea rigs were from Norway. Perhaps more striking has been the passive response of much of British industry. Of the fifty-five exploration platforms operating or on order in the spring of 1974, only seven were to be built by British concerns. Thirty-two are to come from American yards. Of forty-four production platforms, just two are to be constructed in Britain.

The situation on pipelines is even more indicative of major British shortcomings. Perhaps the most powerful illustration of this is the Ekofisk pipeline which is to bring the first oil to the UK from Norwegian fields. The consortium that built it, including Philips, Aquitaine and Norsk Hydro, contains no British partici-pant. The steel for the pipeline itself is Japanese and West German. And from Nigg Bay, near Inverness, where the Texas company Brown and Root has taken main responsibility for the construction of a giant rig, to the Humber, the story appears to be the same. In one sense the exploitation of Britain's oil resources has become a model of international co-operation. It has also been very largely an indication of inadequate British response to a crucial challenge. In 1973, as a result, over £540 million in oil-related investments flowed into the United Kingdom from foreign firms; a boost to the balance of payments in the short term, but a rapidly growing mortgage for the future.

### Oil as collateral

The third illusion, and in our view possibly the most damaging by dint of its psychological dimension, has been the belief that offshore oil riches can serve as financial collateral, or security, for the considerable volume of current borrowing needed to avoid something approaching national bankruptcy in the years up to 1980. The most optimistic argue that the "non-oil" deficit, that is, the trade deficit that is due to imports of goods other than oil—will disappear by the end of 1975, that the oil deficit itself should be eliminated by 1977, and that by 1980 a surplus on Britain's oil account—the result of self-sufficiency in oil because of North Sea supplies—will allow for repayments of all the interest and debts incurred in the meantime. For heavy borrowing by Britain is a certainty over the next five years. In our opinion these assumptions are far from true.

Confidence in loans from the newly rich oil producers as a semi-permanent source of large-scale finance seems misplaced. Some two-thirds of the £2 billion deficit piled up in the first half of 1974 has been financed by a combination of an inflow of oil money (some £400 million), public sector borrowing (£500 million) and loans obtained by public authorities (£400 million). Britain has certainly been successful so far in attracting oil-producer funds, but with the worsening of Britain's economic situation that money may go elsewhere. In addition, Britain may find it increasingly difficult to borrow from other developed countries or from the International Monetary Fund.

More pertinently, in our view, one has to distinguish between national borrowing for present consumption (which is the case for Britain at the moment) and borrowing for investment. Borrowing for present consumption to cushion the present internal consequences of low output and high inflation is no better than securing an overdraft that cannot be repaid and which is not used to improve stocks of manufacturing capacity. In this sense such borrowing is merely a charge on future generations.*

Even when borrowing on the present scale is, at least in part, used for new investment, it will need to yield rates of return as high as, if not higher than, the costs of the loan to justify itself. And these costs are inflated by world conditions and by growing competition for new funds. As has been shown in earlier sections of this study, there is no guarantee that rates of return in British industry will reach those levels without considerable improvements in productivity, labour relations and efficiency. The interest charges on British borrowing, meanwhile, are high and increasing all the time. With each delay in developing the North Sea, whether because of adverse weather, the breakdown of supply timetables by industry, or because of popular pressures to slow down the rate of extraction, certainly a decision under consideration in Norway, Britain's ability to honour the debts it is incurring by "selling North Sea oil forward" will increasingly be called into question. It is often argued, for example, that the interest on government loans is far below the potential value of North Sea production by 1976. This optimistic view unfortunately ignores the uncertain state of current British economics and politics, and the accumulated failures of British industry to respond. For in the absence of dominant involvement in North Sea development by British nationals and a tough government policy on taxes and royalties, the supposed medium-term benefits of the North Sea will accrue very largely to foreigners, as it long did for, say, Abu Dhabi.

*M. W. Corden and Peter Oppenheimer, *Basic Implications of the Rise in Oil Prices*, Trade Policy Research Centre, London, 1974. At least 75 per cent of development capital for the North Sea is being raised abroad, most of it in non-sterling currencies, which has implications for the longer-term status of the pound.

In terms of the balance of payments, both the non-oil and purely oil-related deficits are going to be far more persistent than much British informed opinion seems to think. As has been made clear in an earlier chapter, poor export performance, price inelasticity and income elasticity of imports, and other lesser factors combine to make it unlikely that Britain's competitive position will improve or her payments deficit disappear over the five years ahead. In 1973 the non-oil deficit was a very high £1140 million, and in 1974 could reach £1600 million if not more. From 1975 it may diminish but will remain substantial when compared to levels in other developed economies.

A distinct air of unreality also prevails in discussion of the future evolution of the deficit on imported oil, a requirement which will progressively disappear as it is replaced by Britain's own off-shore reserves. To begin with, it is unlikely that Britain will be totally self-sufficient by 1980, although some part of the import bill will by then have been eliminated. Although local production will be very high by that time, the scheduled levels of output are probably too optimistic. In the first place, it cannot be assumed that imports of equipment for North Sea exploration, crucial if those levels are to be attained, will continue to be financed automatically, that is, by foreign borrowing. Nor should it be taken for granted that even the government will be able to borrow on behalf of development contractors, should private sources of finance become scarce. The Euro-markets are nervous, and bankers are increasingly unwilling to lend at such long term to needy governments while borrowing on such short term from the oil states. And it remains somewhat questionable whether British governments can continue to inspire the confidence abroad necessary to raise the funds required to meet Britain's growing deficits. Already current estimates are of a 1980 financial burden for oil development of £10-14,000 million, which would require annual interest payments by Britain of some £1,000 million.

Table 18.    **Probable Evolution of Britain's Oil Deficit 1973-80**

(National Institute estimates)

£ millions

| | 1973 | 1974 | 1975 | | 1980* | |
|---|---|---|---|---|---|---|
| | | | Year | Second Half (annual rate) | A | B |
| Imports of Crude Oil (f.o.b.) | −939 | −3235 | −3017 | −2198 | −850 | −1250 |
| North Sea Production (mn. tons) | — | — | 4 | 6½ | 108 | 98 |

Source: NIESR Review August 1974, p. 17.
*Assuming that UK oil demand rises by 5 per cent per annum, that oil prices rise by 5 per cent per annum 1976-80 and that profits are £0.4 per barrel in 1975-76 and rise thereafter by 5 per cent per annum.
Column A: North Sea output is 108 million tons per annum.
Column B: North Sea output is 98 million tons per annum.

Future increases in oil extraction costs can only accentuate these factors. And these costs will inevitably rise steeply over the next five years. In doing so they would only be conforming to an established pattern of cost inflation that has dogged other projects of comparable scope: Concorde, Rolls-Royce RB-211 engines, the US F-111, the Channel Tunnel scheme. North Sea operations have been no exception to this principle of rocketing costs. The BP Forties Field, for instance, was costed at £360 million in 1972, and by late 1974 at £630 million. Such levels of escalation are widespread, with smaller exploration groups becoming particularly vulnerable to cash flow problems. But the implications for the longer-term viability of the North Sea fields would be immense, in contrast, say, to Concorde, where overall costs are small by comparison and where any technology fallout will at least go directly to the British and French co-developers. If costs continue to escalate in the North Sea, its oil could be rendered uncompetitive in world terms even without the small drop in prices that we foresee. Reducing such cost increases will be difficult and perhaps can only be achieved by reducing the extraction to a more measured rate than the frantic activity of recent years. That, at least, would allow for the progressive introduction of new offshore technologies in the 1980s with their advantages in efficiency and cost. For, though North Sea oil is of high quality, its value will only stand in relation to competitive alternative sources. While it is now regarded as a timely *deus ex machina*, a helping hand from God, its actual benefits are far less clear.

Thus oil and soaring revenues from the North Sea will not solve Britain's economic ills. The true costs and benefits of this undertaking are being obscured by wishful thinking, and certainly by 1980 no appreciable difference will have been made to Britain's financial standing. The current balance of payments position is the worst in this century, and the economy as a whole is not simply stagnating but actually declining in size. Despite the obvious long-term payment benefits of having a local oil supply, such good fortune cannot be transformed into concrete manufacturing capacity, higher productivity or improved technology and communications without a concerted investment programme. If, as we have suggested, North Sea oil continues to be exploited primarily by foreign capital, then self-sufficiency in oil will not even help raise the British standard of living. In other words, abundant oil, at whatever price, does not, as if by magic, transform outmoded economic and social structures. It is at best a fortunate adjunct to serious economic policies. And without such policies Britain would be no better placed than, say, an oil-producing economy in the Mediterranean or Middle East, with considerable development problems of its own. Britain would then risk becoming Europe's first Trucial State.

# CHAPTER V
## ASSETS THAT HAVE BEEN WASTED

Britain is a nation with formidable assets as well as the troubling liabilities we have already discussed. The strengths of the society are so obvious that one is tempted to ignore them in a book such as this. Europeans and Americans have every reason to know and to be grateful for the tenacity of the British and the stability of Britain's political institutions. The country's parliamentary system has been the envy of troubled Europe. The competence, intellectual quality, and integrity of Britain's civil service have made it virtually without equal. The level of formal scholarship and the quality of British university research and discussion are also probably without real equivalent abroad. Yet despite these assets, and others, the economic troubles of the country persist and deepen. Even British technology, which has been in the first rank of innovation, and the manifest commercial talents of the country, seem in practice to prove irrelevant to the nation's problems. Somehow they are not deployed properly; there seems to be an inability to make these advantages serve great economic and social purposes. Despite an extraordinary tradition in science and technology, British innovations seem to have to go elsewhere to be exploited, to be applied, and manufactured. Despite having produced the greatest economists of the last two centuries, Britain finds its economy mismanaged. These are persistent failures; and it is difficult not to believe that the sources for these failures lie in part in social and cultural factors exceedingly difficult to cure. In the conclusions to this book we will propose some institutional changes which seem to us capable of having a long-range effect on these matters and which may help in putting the obvious talents of British society to work in the practical task of improving the standard of life for the mass of the British. It will be useful also to examine two cases in which it is very clear that major assets of Britain have been wasted. These are education and the management of the regional resources of the country.

### Education: reform and resistance

That British education prior to the coronation of Victoria was geared to the maintenance of a social and economic *status quo* is widely recognised. In such parts of England as Yorkshire, regions of industrial and commercial expansion, nonconformist manufacturers, still denied places at Oxford and Cambridge by a resistance to "vulgar men of trade", established and supported their own quite separate schools. The more energetic amongst the working classes founded their own Young Men's Improvement Societies, providing mechanical training to those ill-fitted by background or means for the supposedly refined heights of university education. Primary education was practically non-existent in the early 19th century. Before 1870 a town such as Huddersfield, for instance, in the heart of industrial England, spent nothing at all on public education.*

---

*B. Jackson and D. Marsden, *Education and the Working Class* (Pelican, 1966).

Even then there were, it is true, certain notions about the future social and institutional structure Britain would need in an industrial age, but they usually reflected the interests of groups anxious to maintain an economic and political power that was theirs by long tradition, but which was now under challenge from those within the new entrepreneurial and manufacturing classes. Revisions in the educational system tended to guarantee the continuation of a particular kind of society. The public schools, long synonymous with landed privilege, were given the new role of providing the sons of commerce with an education conforming to the gentlemanly ideal. The university system, still little more than an heir of ecclesiasticism and which in 1850 rested almost entirely on Oxford and Cambridge, at that time, to echo an eminent commentator, dreamily "sleeping behind their ancient statutes", was to be a training ground for the new industrial élite; but in fact they were to make only a reluctant deference to the practical demands of modern economic management. Education was tied firmly to the notion of privilege, and amongst the wider populace only those prepared to take initiative to provide themselves with teaching could hope to break out of a circle of ignorance and poorly developed skills.

The innovations of the 1870s did little to change this. At the core of these reforms lay the subtle, but telling, distinction that was made between education for technical and scientific facility on the one hand, and grooming for power on the other; a distinction that still underpins the structure of British higher education.

That this distinction was based principally on the issue of class would be of rather less significance had it not been that it gave further impetus to the separation of the technician and his skills from the mainstream of establishment influence that a comparatively rigid class system had generated in the early years of industrial change a century or more before. The working class Society simply became the technical college of today. When the provincial universities sprang up after 1880—Birmingham, Wales, Manchester's Victoria University, as well as new colleges added to London—they were seen, not as heirs of the traditions of Oxbridge, but rather as working-class cousins, extemporising concessions to a pressing national need for scientists and engineers. This introduction of class into the dissemination and application of science was to become a hallmark of British practice, setting it apart from those other countries rapidly establishing their own technological bases. As Matthew Arnold, in his capacity as a school inspector, was moved to observe, on the eve of the 1870s:

> So we have amongst us the spectacle of a middle class cut in two and in a way unexampled anywhere else, of a professional class brought up on the first plane, with fine and governing qualities, but without the idea of science; while that immense business class, which is becoming so important a power in all countries, on which the future so depends . . . is in England brought up on the second plane, cut off from the aristocracy and the professions, and without governing qualities.*

*Quoted in Michael Fores, "Britain's Economic Growth and the 1870 Watershed", *Lloyd's Bank Review*, January 1971.

In the century that has followed little has been done to eliminate this distinction, or to make British education draw upon the national community as a whole to obtain the technologists and managers that any radically transformed economic system requires. Even the Education Act of 1944, hailed as an example of egalitarian legislation, was to succumb to the inexorable pressures of social forces that proved stronger than mere laws. The major beneficiaries of expanded and improved secondary education after 1944 were the children of the middle classes, not the less privileged that had hitherto manned the factories and farms. A decade after the passage of the Education Act only 8500 pupils from the so-called "modern" schools sat the examinations for the all-important Certificate of Education, while the traditional grammar schools and public schools between them provided a total of some 186,000 candidates.* A consolidated pattern of early leaving, a product of poor school facilities and straitened home circumstances, manifested the signal failure of the 1944 Act to broaden the opportunities open to working-class children. In this respect a poor British performance in deepening the base of its higher education simply reinforced the propensity of the educational system to entrench social differences before the onset of the employment cycle.

### Education for what?

Matthew Arnold certainly made perceptive comment on the real nature of British education in the 1860s and 1870s, but he also put his finger on a crucial facet of Victorian upper-class attitudes, namely the unease before the technological challenge of advanced industrialism. The engineer, despite the fact that he built the railways, bridges and iron ships that had taken Britain's influence to the furthest corners of the globe, was nevertheless viewed as an adjunct to the factory process. As Michael Fores has pointed out, only civil engineers appear as a professional group in official statistics and censuses up to 1881; and even the civil engineers adopted the snobbish habits of high Victorianism, ignoring the obvious abilities of George Stephenson, for example, on the grounds that his semi-literate presence did not fit their gentlemanly ways.†

This ostracism of the technologist reflected an unconsidered but powerful assumption that, in fact, the future of British society somehow lay, not in meeting the challenge set by German or American inventors and scientists, but in embellishing and refining the genteel qualities of the British way of life. That, in other words, Britain's future could best be secured by encouraging technological advance within the strict bounds of a traditional order; the true purpose of education was seen as jeopardised by a clamour for crude scientific progress.

This attitude was still evident as late as the Plowden Report on education, which appeared after lengthy researches in 1967. In a few lines the consequences of the accumulated misconceptions of British educational philosophy were spelt out:

*E. J. Hobsbawm, *Industry and Empire* (Penguin 1969) p. 287.
†Fores, op. cit.

84

Comparisons with other countries—all of them more recently industrialised than Britain but all now at a similar stage of economic development—suggest that we have not done enough to provide the educational background necessary to support an economy which needs fewer and fewer unskilled workers and increasing numbers of skilled and adaptable people.*

This was more than a statement of haphazard comparative fact: it was above all an allusion to the impractical élitism that gave rise to the separation of technology from pure learning and hence to the downgrading of the status of the scientist. The place of the scientist in a society still largely governed by the creed of social station was inevitably to be one of service to an ideal of genteel governance. Science was regarded as a necessary but not primary factor in the economic system and thus it was not to be allowed to divert educational practice from its essential role of educating for rank.

While traditional British educational practice provided a formidable defence of the classical and humane studies and of scholarship as a civilising force, this essential task was accomplished by making a humane education the prerogative of a social class. A drastic line was drawn on an irrelevant criterion between education and scholarship on the one hand and the practical employment of human knowledge in the affairs of society on the other. Pure science was admitted to the great universities; technology and engineering were consigned to schools whose social inferiority was unmistakable. In short, a legitimate intellectual distinction between learning pursued for its own sake and learning applied to social and economic ends was made into a social distinction that set off an élite from the rest. This did violence to the mind; scholarship, to say nothing of wisdom, is not class-restricted. But it also had pernicious effects upon the society and economy of the country. Those who actually applied knowledge in the ordinary life of the country were made to feel the inferiority of their rôle.

**British education today**

Britain today educates too few people, and for the wrong subjects. The size of the university enrolment, despite high public spending, is one of the smallest in the industrialised world, and reflects the widespread belief in British educational circles in concentrated quality and smallness of student numbers, two objectives, which are not necessarily interdependent. This belief results in turn not only from the tradition of seeing education as a guardian of the hierarchy of opportunity but from inadequate attention at the broader planning level to exactly what the longer term aim of educational policy should be.

As Table 22 demonstrates, comparisons with other advanced industrial countries are highly unfavourable for England and Wales and even more so for Scotland.

*A Report of the Central Advisory Council for Education (England). Vol. I, HMSO 1967 pp. 50-55.

While at the age of sixteen, for example, 58 per cent of Belgian children are at school, only 35 per cent of English children and 30 per cent of Scottish have the same opportunity. At seventeen, disparities are even more glaring.

Table 22

**Staying on at school**

| Compulsory education age limits | Year | Children at school as percentage of the age group | |
|---|---|---|---|
| | | 16 | 17 |
| United Kingdom | | | |
| England and Wales 5–15 | 1966–67 | 35 | 21 |
| Scotland 5–15 | 1966–67 | 30 | 17 |
| Belgium 6–14 | 1965 | 58 | 44 |
| France 6–16 | 1967–68 | 55 | 41 |
| Germany (Fed. Rep.) 6–15/18 | 1965 | 27 | 17 |
| Italy 6–14 | 1965–66 | 34 | 27 |
| Netherlands 7–15 | 1967–68 | 51 | 31 |
| Luxembourg 6–15 | 1967–68 | 39 | 27 |
| USA. 6/7/8–16/17/18 | 1964–66 | 93 | 76 |
| Japan 6–15 | 1964 | 60 | 57 |

*Source:* Social Trends III, HMSO 1972.

The experience of the 1960s, the decade of the Robbins Report, provides an example of this. The terms of reference of the Robbins Committee were quite clearly focused on future needs: "to review the pattern of higher full-time education in Great Britain and in the light of national needs and resources to advise Her Majesty's Government on what principles its long-term development should be based."[*]

Yet the results of the Committee's work reflected the significant argument, "that the supply of places should be based on the demand for places from potential entrants, rather than on the demand in the economy for the products of higher education."[†]

In other words, population growth and individual proclivity would be the basis used to plot future university expansion, rather than any structured programme for generating graduates for the future needs of society or the economy. The quantitative recommendations of the Committee that resulted from this approach were immediately accepted by the government of the day and published in a White Paper which appeared within twenty-four hours of the report itself.

[*] Cmnd. 2154 HMSO 1963.

[†] R. Layard, J. King and C. Moser, *The Impact of Robbins* (Penguin 1969) p. 21.

Chart XXI

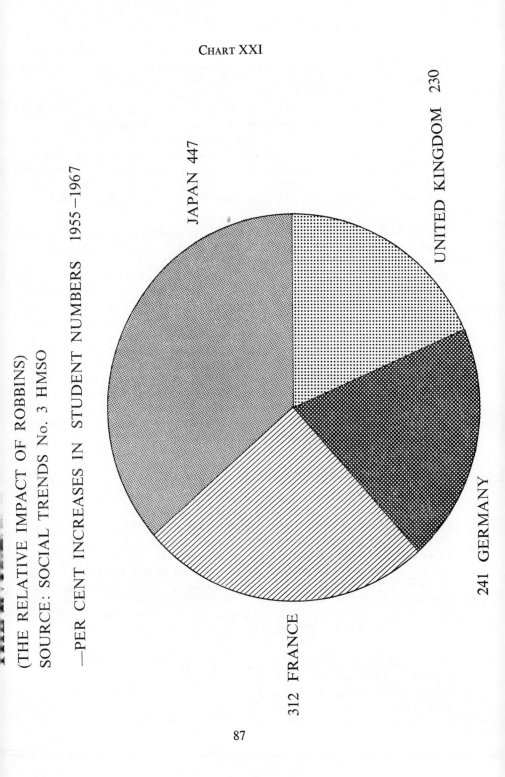

(THE RELATIVE IMPACT OF ROBBINS)
SOURCE: SOCIAL TRENDS No. 3 HMSO

—PER CENT INCREASES IN STUDENT NUMBERS 1955–1967

JAPAN 447

UNITED KINGDOM 230

241 GERMANY

312 FRANCE

During the 1960s Britain's graduate base did expand. It grew by some 50 per cent over the decade. But in comparison to economies of similar size and structure like France, Italy, and Japan* it actually fell even further behind, for these other countries, too, had their own expansion programmes. By the time the Robbins proposals had taken full effect in 1967-8, the UK had a proportionately smaller university population than any other comparable nation, and had experienced the slowest historical rate of growth in student numbers. Yet the limitation on expanding university places was not a practical necessity; Sir John Wolfenden, Chairman of the University Grants Committee, was told by the universities themselves on the morrow of Robbins' report that they could have provided at least 20,000 places *more* than the 197,000 asked for.†

The eventual impact of Robbins' proposals was a simple and modest increase in student numbers. This helped meet the upsurge in A-level candidates caused by the birth-rate rise of the early post-war period; and in fact meeting this upsurge seems to have been the main objective of the Committee without any accompanying re-orientation of syllabuses or degree structure. For the late 1960s there was a strong swing away from science at A-level and in university preferences: between 1961 and 1967 the number of those specialising in arts subjects increased by 114 per cent, those in science by only 52 per cent. It was a trend the Committee decided to ignore. In the words of researchers who had actually been responsible for the statistical basis of the Committee's work, "[the shift] was first noticed in the Robbins Report, but, perhaps unfortunately, no forecast was made of its future course."‡ Consequently, one of the potentially most vital reforms of university education in the United Kingdom since the growth of the provincial universities in the 1880s became a haphazard response to a bulge in the national population curve.

**The lack of an educational strategy**

There has been a failure to come to grips with the strategic purposes of British education; this was comprehensively exhibited in the Robbins Report and in the official reactions to it. The University Grants Committee, responsible for the orientation of university spending, decided that no determined policy on expansion of science and technology was necessary. In November 1967, in the wake of Robbins, the Committee formally announced that the major increase in university places must be in arts subjects rather than in science. One significant consequence was a severe restriction in the expected growth of the old colleges of advanced technology, which were later to be incorporated into the university system proper and hence affected by the general limitation of science studies.§

---

* West Germany is the exception.
† *The Impact of Robbins*, p. 41.
‡ *The Impact of Robbins*, p. 45.
§ Ibid, p. 47.

The disconcerting aspect of this official acceptance of a weakening science sector in higher education is that it did not follow from a rational reappraisal of national educational objectives. That, at least, would have been a realistic procedure. But the decision to allow expansion of the non-science university intake flowed almost entirely from the complexion of the output from the secondary schools, whose curricula were not agreed in consultation with the universities that were eventually to absorb their products. There was no effort, that is, to alter the distribution of university intake in greater favour of science and technology, a decision that was soundly condemned by bodies such as the Council for Scientific Policy, who urged that the swing against technical subjects be halted and reversed.*

In some respects this failure to provide a more ambitious programme for science teaching at the upper levels reflected a confused official outlook on science policy in general. At the level of applied science in the industrial field, for example, there has never existed a co-ordinated view of the longer-term purposes of the national scientific effort, or of how it might interlock with national economic planning. As Dr. Ieuan Maddock, Chief Scientist at the Department of Trade and Industry, was to put it in October this year: "it will be a major step forward if we can fashion a proper research policy, because in the past our programmes have just been a huge rag-bag."†

The failure to expand the teaching of science subjects also sprang from a lack of compatability between the changing demands of modern economic life and the way children were being taught in Britain's schools. This incompatibility became most noticeable in the training of teachers. As Michael Duane was to observe, in a survey of teacher training:

If ever there was an area in education almost totally lacking in coherent form, befuddled and contradictory in its theories and chronically incompetent in relating practice to precept, then it can be seen in that part of education concerned with the training of teachers . . . since the last war as job-mobility increased through the introduction of new machines, new materials and new forms of organisation and control, teachers have found themselves more and more at a loss *what* to teach. They have, therefore, been thrown back on the idea of educating 'for leisure', or 'for life' rather than simply 'for work'.‡

Hence, from teachers to university graduates there seemingly has developed an incompatibility of ends and means. Teaching has continued in the traditional furrow with very little provision for the administrative and technological demands of tomorrow, in contrast, say, to the originating purpose of the *grandes écoles* and l'Ecole Nationale d'Administration in France.

* *Enquiry into the Flow of Candidates in Science and Technology into Higher Education*, Cmnd. 3541.

† *Sunday Telegraph*, 13 October, 1974.

‡ M. Duane, "The Training of Teachers", *Education and Training*, Vol. 10, No. 3.

**The gap between education and work**

By the beginning of the 1970s signs of the recent weaknesses in university preparation began to appear. Graduates began to be diverted into fringe employment or into work for which they were not schooled as undergraduates. By 1972-3 only 12 per cent of the 65,000 non-medical graduates coming out of Britain's universities entered careers in industry, a drop from the previous year and a continuation of a falling trend dating from the beginning of the 1960s.* By early 1974 the Department of Employment was prompted to conclude that a major problem of graduate unemployment loomed in the early 1980s as a result of inadequate linkage between university output and changes in the economy. There will be, by 1980, double the total number of graduates that there were in the mid-1960s, about 1,400,000. This growth in the number of qualified people has not been matched by a corresponding demand for people with these qualifications. In other words, even a modest future growth in the student population will not avoid a growing shortfall between graduate numbers and employment opportunities. It seems increasingly probable that the British graduate of the 1980s will find himself required to seek inappropriate work in such fields as supermarket management, factory floor supervision, or insurance sales because he has not received a formation that is relevant to the contemporary needs of the British economy. This situation will become particularly acute if women graduates, traditionally obliged to take up employment as glorified secretaries or underpaid research assistants, exert a new influence on the graduate market and capture jobs traditionally going to males.†

It was to be expected, therefore, that some reaction would set in through the operation of exactly those forces of supply and demand upon which the Robbins Committee rested so much faith a decade ago. The prospect of irrelevant qualifications or inadequate opportunity in the Britain of 1980 is already one factor having an effect on undergraduate intake. During 1973, the level of applications for university places was almost 10 per cent lower than in 1972, and because of the switch away from sciences at secondary school level, this fall has been most concentrated in scientific and technical subjects. Engineering and technology departments admitted only 82 students for every 100 places available, science departments only 84. Arts and languages filled over 90 per cent of their vacancies. In the meantime admissions of students from abroad have grown over nine times as fast, at about 15 per cent each year.‡

This slackening in demand for university education combined with the restrictions on new university building imposed at the beginning of the 1970s, make it very probable that by the end of this decade Britain will have a smaller university programme than any other Western country of similar size and economic

* *First Destination of University Graduates 1971-1972*, the Annual Report of the Central Services Unit for University Careers.
† *Employment Prospects for the Highly Qualified*, Department of Employment, May 1974.
‡ Universities Central Council on Admissions (UCCA) *Eleventh Report 1972-1973*.

structure. Estimates of the Committee of Vice-Chancellors and Principals are of a university population in the late 1970s of 275,000, considerably below the 306,000 originally planned and less, even, than the 293,000 foreseen by the University Council for admissions.* What is more, due to a relative failure to adjust educational priorities to changes or projected changes in the economy at large, these students will increasingly be studying the wrong subjects, or training for out-moded functions.

### The problem of Britain's regions

British regional development has reflected weaknesses of economic management that have been observable at the broader national level. Despite enormous financial expenditures and devotion of considerable manpower to the problems of Britain's regions, viewed as a whole the situation is worse now than it was a generation ago.† For although British concern for conditions and opportunities in the disadvantaged regions has a long history, the Special Areas Act of 1934 being one of Europe's first official actions in the regional field, there has never been developed a structured policy of regional incentives based on an integrated national plan with a guaranteed life-span of, say, twenty-five years.

For the most part British regional planning has been merely an extension of standard macro-economics. The "region" has been treated as a miniature national economy, notwithstanding the unreality of assuming, for instance, that the region could be closed for purposes of analysis as was common in orthodox macro-economic thinking, or of refusing to acknowledge that a region can have a negative rate of growth—for that is clearly possible. What has remained the touchstone of soundness in regional policy has been the level of unemployment: a monument to Keynesianism, perhaps, but also a consequence of unwillingness to create and seek out more relevant indicators of regional conditions.

The point needs to be made that although the revolutionary importance of the cyclical control measures elaborated by J. M. Keynes in the 1930s should not be underestimated, their emphasis on unemployment as the critical criterion in directing corrective policies has tended to obscure the significance of other factors in the regional economies. Thus British regional policy has been rigidly tied to a theory of economic management unsuited to the more complex problems of an internationalised and rapidly changing economic environment of the present day.

It was inevitable that national policies thus dominated by economists and statisticians would place little weight on such factors as the geographic and

---

*The Times, 18 October, 1974.

†By 1973/1974 annual spending on regional assistance totalled about £250 million, *Industrial and Regional Development*, Cmnd. 4942 HMSO.

topographic attributes of a region, or any special characteristics of neighbouring regions or sea regions or sea zones that might bear on the future of a specific problem area. As a specialist on regional development put it recently:

"Economists have been reluctant to accept that there is any regularity in the spatial organisation of the economy . . . they liked smooth curves which were amenable to calculus, while distance functions and other spatial parameters tended to exhibit inconvenient discontinuities . . . analysis of distance and the spatial distribution of people and activities was felt to be the province of the geographers, a breed for whom economists have never had a high regard."*

Thus assistance went primarily to regions with the highest unemployment, without any serious attempt to assess the longer-term impact of that assistance, or the alternatives to such action, or indeed the effects that this assistance might have in regions close by that did not themselves benefit directly. In short, there seemed to be no attempt to chart a new industrialising course involving highly capital-intensive processes or advanced technology, and even less interest was shown in a strategy for the remodelling of the whole national economy incorporating both the traditionally buoyant regions and those long regarded as "depressed".

Hence, in one of the most recent White Papers on regional policy, *Industrial and Regional Development*, it is made clear that the priority industries for regional development grants are precisely those that should progressively be phased out in the interests of improved long-term productivity and employment conditions: mining and quarrying, vehicles, textiles, leather goods, metal manufacture, and so on.

Table 23

**Industries Eligible for Regional Development
Grants under 1972 White Paper provisions**

| | |
|---|---|
| Mining and Quarrying | Vehicles |
| Food, Drink and Tobacco | Metal Goods not elsewhere specified |
| Coal and Petroleum Products | Textiles |
| Chemicals and Allied Industries | Leather, Leather Goods and Fur |
| Metal Manufacture | Clothing and Footwear |
| Mechanical Engineering | Bricks, Pottery, Glass, Cement, etc. |
| Instrument Engineering | Timber, Furniture, etc. |
| Electrical Engineering | Paper, Printing and Publishing |
| Shipbuilding & Marine | Other Manufacturing Industries |
| Engineering | Construction |

*Source: Industrial and Regional Development, Cmnd. 4942.*

*H. W. Richardson, *Elements of Regional Economics*, Penguin Books (London 1969), p. 13.

92

## Weakening the strong regions

The net effect of British policies for industrial revitalisation has included the accentuation of problems in many depressed areas and the absolute weakening and impoverishment of those developed and traditionally successful regions generally seen as the powerhouses of the country's manufacturing capacity. In other words, despite some forty years of official effort in the regional field, there has been continued stagnation in most of those areas picked out for assistance, and the penalising of areas such as the Midlands, where plant has aged and little attempt has been made to shift the bias of local production to forms of activity suited to the competitive requirements of a new generation.

The characteristics of this impact can be gauged by examining a classic depressed region, the North of England, and comparing its evolution to that of the Midlands, the most industrialised, and still one of the most prosperous, parts of the United Kingdom.

The North, of course, is confronted with the legacy of the early industrialisation of Britain. It has a history of coal mining, shipbuilding and engineering—those industries, in fact, which have suffered most from the national economic decline. It is little surprise that it was the home of the Jarrow marchers. Today it has more of its region covered by Special Development Area status, a reference to the acuteness of its economic problems, than any other British region with the exception of Scotland, which, as we shall argue below, actually has more favourable prospects. The North of England constitutes a microcosm of the general economic condition. Significantly, it has the regional economic structure most comparable to the national norm: it is Britain's average region.

As a major depressed area it has received considerable public assistance. It has shown the highest annual average growth rate for public fixed capital formation of any British region in recent years. But public aid is not sufficient as a stimulus for regional growth, any more than it is for the country as a whole. Public investment needs to fit into a generally dynamic climate: of innovation in plant, of imaginative interventions by the private sector industries. But this climate has not emerged. Outside purely officially administered investment in building and works, the performance in other types of investment has been appalling. Private investment in plant and machinery, the key to long-term economic health in a mixed economy, actually *declined absolutely* from 1965, while the total stock of fixed capital, comprising both private and public expenditure on capital formation, expanded at less than half the national average rate. The aggregate effect of this neglect was a regional rate of growth for output as a whole that was the lowest in the United Kingdom over the decade of the 1960s.

Yet the Midlands fared little better, although for more complex reasons. In the absence of any global strategy that placed specific regional funding within a comprehensive plan for bringing about regional change in the economy as a whole, assisting Britain's "depressed" regions has meant total neglect of those regions thought to be well-endowed and permanently viable. There was a failure at the official level to appreciate that even industrialised regions need to be competently planned and have provision made for their future orientation.

As a recent press analysis has pointed out, new plant investment is unlikely to be profitable in the long-term in the United Kingdom in sectors such as steel, shipbuilding, most consumer electronics and domestic appliances, most machine tools, and a larger proportion of petro-chemicals production than many of us wish to concede.* More specifically, British car manufacturing plants, for instance, will face increasing competition in terms of price, quality and delivery performance from countries now moving into this particular phase of their development cycles: Spain, increasingly Brazil, Mexico and Iran.† Lacking a revolution in the technology of vehicle productions, new investment in motor vehicle plant in the United Kingdom for production in the 1980s, even given improved labour management relations, will tend increasingly to be profitable only if the labour force will accept the living and working standards of its new rivals in Southern Europe or Latin America—which it obviously will not. Continental Northern Europe has thus far been able to maintain the competitiveness of its own vehicle plants by importing several million migrant workers from Europe's Mediterranean and African fringes which helped fill serious gaps in the local labour reserve (though it did not lower wage costs) and by lowering its profit margins. But these are practices that cannot be kept up indefinitely, and eventually there must be a much-reduced European motor industry.

The implications of such a change for a region such as the Midlands, with a sixth of its industrial work force employed directly in vehicle production and many of the remainder dependent upon its secondary requirements, are quite clearly profound. In the absence of any investment strategy for the Midlands that is designed to permit the region to survive the economic demise of industries like that of motor vehicles, such a shift in the global structure of manufacturing could be disastrous.

Such strategies have not emerged. There is not, in any event, any real allowance for them in current regional policy, and the record of regional investment and productivity clearly shows that the Midlands, wrongly taken as an example of regional health, has suffered immensely from being ignored. From 1965 the West Midlands' share of UK investment has fallen steadily in all sectors, and in the seven categories of investment adopted by the West Midlands County Council in its planning, the region attained levels below the national average in six. In the seventh category, that of public investment in plant and machinery, the West Midlands' growth rate was a miniscule 0.2 per cent yearly.

*The Economist, 28 April, 1973.

†By 1980 production of vehicles in each of these countries will probably range between 500,000 and 1,000,000 annually.

Its share of UK public investment in new construction has fallen steadily since the 1960s. Its rate of unemployment has risen sharply from a buoyant 50 per cent of the nation's average for much of the 1950s and 1960s to above 90 per cent, in 1972. And as the most industrialised of Britain's regions, the West Midlands bears the brunt of any centrally imposed policies of restraint or deflation. Significantly, during the three-day week imposed in December 1973, unemployment in the area leapt by 563 per cent in comparison to a UK average of just over 200 per cent.* The manufacturing capacity of the region is the most specialised in Britain, and is therefore the most vulnerable to changes. It has, too, the highest percentage of small firms. It is, in almost every way, the workshop of Britain, and it suffers disproportionately as the country's fortunes alter.

As a consequence, the Midlands has seen its economic strength sapped as its productive capacity lost its earlier efficiency, and its levels of prosperity—in the 1950s undoubtedly among Europe's highest—gradually fall behind Europe's. More recently, its prosperity has dropped behind that of many British regions. In all probability the Midlands as a whole will be one of Britain's, and certainly Europe's, poorer areas in the 1980s.

### The Scottish exception

Britain's regional policies have simply accentuated the failures exhibited by national economic management, first by expecting historically productive regions to fend for themselves in the midst of general stagnation, and second by not ensuring that the kind of investment moving into "depressed" regions, through incentives or official initiative, generates self-sustaining regional growth.

At the level of incomes this eventually produces increasing distortions between regions which have an inherent capacity to expand economically and those which do not. The London area, for instance, because of the weight of commercial activity centred there, and because of the concentration of indigenous wealth that London's status as a cultural and financial hub has produced, has fared well in the liberal, *laissez-faire* climate of Britain's industrial policies over the years. Instead of the gap between the London region and the country as a whole narrowing (as it might have done if public action had stimulated economic life in the poorer areas) the South-East is steadily drawing away from the remainder of the country. By the early 1980s general levels of income in London and the Home Counties could be so different from those in most parts of the United Kingdom as a whole that the region would almost become a separate economy in its own right, with commercial and cultural habits based on a prosperity quite unknown in the country at large.

*A Time For Action, a discussion document prepared by the West Midlands County Council, September 1974.

There is, nevertheless, a notable exception to this general pattern, for the Scottish economy is likely to experience a similar level of expansion to that of the London area over the next decade. Contrary to a notion prevalent certainly during the late 1960s, and persisting even today, Scotland is no longer a nation of crofters, whisky distillers and derelict dockyards.

The Scottish economy has since the early 1960s experienced one of the highest rates of growth in regional output in Britain as well as the highest rate of growth in incomes per head of any part of the United Kingdom. This has meant that by the end of the 1960s incomes per head in Scotland were approaching the national average, after generations of income levels lower than any part of the country with the exception of Ireland. This was a reversal of a long standing relationship, one aptly summed up by the historian E. J. Hobsbawm in the following words. "Compared with England, all Scotland was economically backward, and above all poor. In 1750 the prosperous Scotsman ate more simply, was housed worse, and possessed fewer household goods than Englishmen of more modest standing, and rich Scotsmen—at least by southern standards—hardly existed outside the small ranks of the landed aristocracy."*

It was still possible in 1960 to say that Scotland was, with Northern Ireland, the poorest part of the Kingdom, with general levels of income some 22 per cent lower than those in Britain's South-East or Midlands. Yet high and sustained economic growth was eroding that difference even before the discoveries of offshore oil after 1965.

By the beginning of the 1970s incomes had risen considerably. In average terms they were higher than in any other region with the exception of London, the Midlands and the industrialised North West of England. The upsurge in oil-related investment, the greater part of it from outside the United Kingdom, that came after about 1970, was further accentuated after the four-fold increase in oil prices imposed by OPEC in the winter of 1973-4. Much of Scotland's rate of expansion had initially stemmed from changes to the geographic balance of the Scottish economy, not least a shift in the centre of gravity to the east and away from the traditionally depressed and structurally outmoded Clydeside. Some of it was the result of conscious changes in the kind of industry Scotland developed: the high-technology products with high value-added now typical of Fife, or the modern aluminium-producing processes exemplified by the smelter plant at Invergordon. It should be stressed that much came from a considerable influx of American capital: after the London area Scotland has attracted more American industry than any other British region—over three times that going into England's depressed North region, for example. And some of the improvements in average income certainly came from the continued emigration of population that Scotland has for long suffered, although it is likely that this will become an increasingly unimportant feature of Scotland's economic profile over the late 1970s.

*Op. cit. p. 300.

CHART XXII

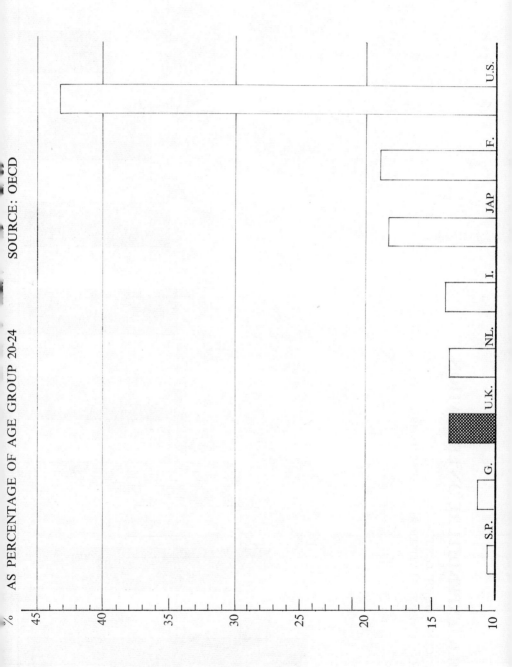

AS PERCENTAGE OF AGE GROUP 20-24    SOURCE: OECD

CHART XXIII

# PUBLIC EXPENDITURE ON EDUCATION

AS PERCENTAGE OF G.N.P.

SOURCE: UNESCO STATISTICAL YEARBOOK 1972

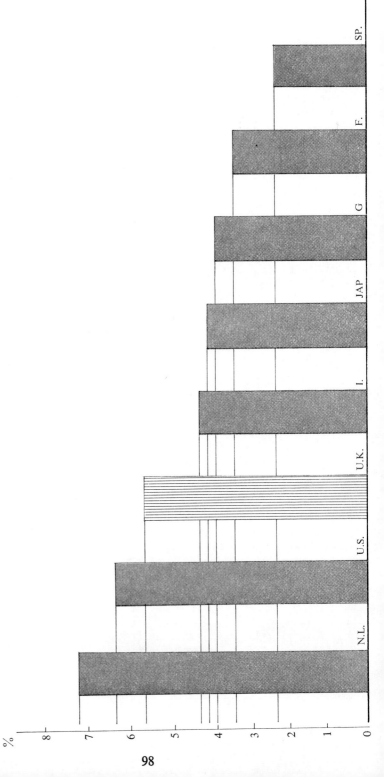

Overall, it is probable that Scotland's new regional dynamism will allow for a steady increase of living standards and social amenities. By the early 1980s Scotland should have a level of prosperity equal to that of the more wealthy parts of the United Kingdom and, more important, would have it based on more modern industries.

Scotland's relative success does not contradict our broader criticisms of Britain's traditional regional development programmes. During the period of rapid Scottish growth after 1965, for example, public fixed capital formation in new buildings and works—a reflection of central government concern for stimulating local economies—rose by only 7.9 per cent each year, considerably below the 16.9 per cent experienced in the North region or even the 15.2 per cent seen in the heavily developed English North-West. Scotland's level of benefit in this sector was even below a national average of 8.8 per cent, and the same was true of private investment in plant and machinery.* In other words, investments made in Scotland on government initiative were below average in volume, and the industries taking advantage of regional incentives to establish themselves there were in a large number of cases non-British. The more likely explanation of Scotland's improved performance lies in the *quality* of the investment that went into Scotland, in its sectoral spread, and in the evenness of its distribution between the various categories of capital spending: vehicles, buildings, plant. These were accompanied by a noticeable shift into different geographic zones that allowed a changed inter-dependency to develop, breaking in some measure the former relationship between employment and those decaying or structurally cumbersome industries for which industrial Scotland became renowned in the text books of economic decline. Scotland's success thus represents one alternative of several for other British regions. Above all it suggests that effective regional changes can also become the foundations for more impressive economic growth.

## Britain's regions and Europe's regions

The future of Britain's economy is as firmly tied to the development of Europe's economy as a whole as it is to shifts in the balance of purely internal elements. But few seem prepared to concede the real extent of changes in the regional balance of the European economy. Part of this reluctance, which is evident in both academic and business spheres, no doubt results from the long drawn-out affair of Britain's entrance into an integrated Europe. The debate on Britain and the Six, which spanned a quarter of a century from the late 1940s, and indeed still goes on, riveted attention on the European economy as it used to be: coal, steel, and heavy industry concentrated in the centre of western Europe. This Europe no longer exists, and the changes that have taken place over the past decade and a half have great implications for the future structure of Britain's economy, not least at the regional level.

---

*cf, *A Time For Action.*

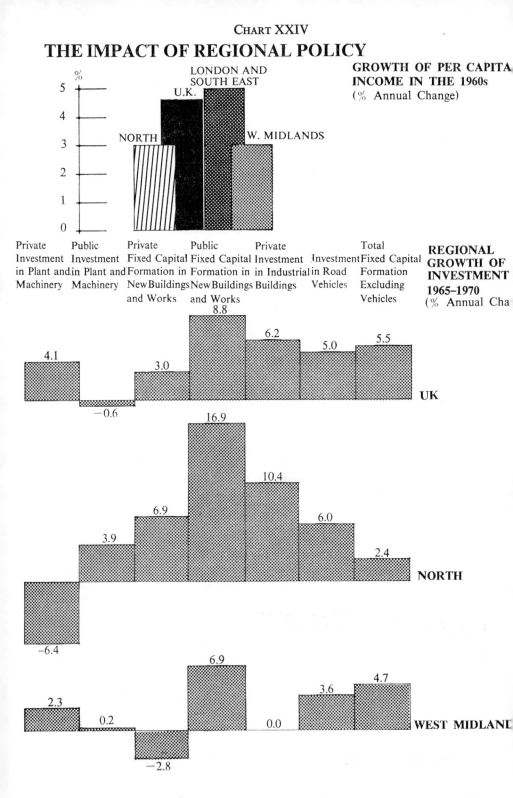

CHART XXIV

# THE IMPACT OF REGIONAL POLICY

LONDON AND SOUTH EAST

U.K.

NORTH

W. MIDLANDS

**GROWTH OF PER CAPITA INCOME IN THE 1960s**
(% Annual Change)

| Private Investment in Plant and Machinery | Public Investment in Plant and Machinery | Private Fixed Capital Formation in New Buildings and Works | Public Fixed Capital Formation in New Buildings and Works | Private Investment in Industrial Buildings | Investment in Road Vehicles | Total Fixed Capital Formation Excluding Vehicles |
|---|---|---|---|---|---|---|

**REGIONAL GROWTH OF INVESTMENT 1965–1970**
(% Annual Cha

UK: 4.1, −0.6, 3.0, 8.8, 6.2, 5.0, 5.5

NORTH: 3.9, −6.4, 6.9, 16.9, 10.4, 6.0, 2.4

WEST MIDLAND: 2.3, 0.2, −2.8, 6.9, 0.0, 3.6, 4.7

SOURCE: WEST MIDLANDS COUNTY COUNCIL AND HUDSON INSTITUTE

Old notions of Europe's economy revolved around the future of its basic industries. The Common Market of the Six grew from the amalgamation of the continent's iron, steel and coal production in 1952 under the framework of the European Coal and Steel Community: output was found in the Ruhr, in the Netherlands, in Belgium and in North France. The textbooks of European integration emphasised that an integrational pull towards this centre provided the Market with its cohesion.

Yet the foundations of Europe's economy were changing even as the Market itself was being formed. Above all, the energy base of its manufacturing industry was shifting from coal to dependence on cheap, more efficient, oil. Over the last decade, while coal output in the United States climbed from 430 million tons annually to above 600 million tons, and in the Soviet Union from 400 million tons to 500 million tons, production in the Six fell from 235 million to 130 million tons yearly. Even the exigencies of the oil price rise in the winter of 1973-4 did not alter this. British coal production, for example, under the revised programme announced in the Summer of 1974, is planned only to maintain its 1974 level into the early 1980s, while French and West German production will continue to fall. One reason why coal could not easily regain its ascendant position was that the continental economy had lost the capacity to use it: it had dispersed geographically or had become geared to supplies of oil, and in most cases a combination of the two.

The fragmentation of the West European economy during the 1960s had two major effects. First, there was an accelerating movement of industry towards coastal zones. Second, there was a more comprehensive shift in the pattern of economic dynamism towards the South of Europe, benefiting especially the Mediterranean economies of Italy, Spain and Southern France.

This *glissement vers la mer*, or drift to the seacoasts, of European industry is readily noticeable in steel production. Recent large developments in steel have been both coastal and Mediterranean: Taranto in Southern Italy, Fos in Southern France and Sagunto, near Valencia, in Spain. Indeed, currently expressed fears about coastal pollution in Western Europe have been primarily linked, not to oil-processing activities, but to the construction of steel plants on coastal sites.

This dispersal of large-scale industry away from Europe's centre, besides reflecting the expansion of the southern economies and the comparative stagnation of those in North-Western Europe, has stemmed from changes in the economics of location and scale. Perhaps the most important single change affecting plant size has been the removal of traditional limits on optimum levels of production. Since the early 1960s, for example, the engineering industry has increased considerably its unit sizes, with constraints coming only from technical barriers, local supply of necessary raw materials, availability of

101

financial resources and transport costs. In other words, there is less emphasis on purely internal marginal costs and returns.

As a result, greater relevance has been attached to factors external to the manufacturing unit itself. Both the geographic diversification of capacity and the enlargement of the West European market overall (a development enhanced by Britain's entry into the European Community) accentuated the role of transfer costs, chiefly transport, in overall competitiveness. Since costs of production were equalising throughout that enlarged market, distance became a major component of eventual price. Geography, in other words, had come to challenge more traditional economic variables.

Such considerations favoured the manufacture of light products through capital-intensive processes which included a high technological component. The transport costs factor especially penalised heavy goods industries. Almost 25 per cent of total costs in industries producing, say, construction materials or relying on bulk raw materials, is absorbed by transport; in large-scale production of household consumer durables the proportion is more like 2 per cent. Those classic basic industries concentrated in the central area of the continent which had formed the original economic rationale for European integration have been handicapped as a result. Whereas during the inter-war period and in the 1950s the special characteristics of the Rhine provided the Ruhr and the Netherlands with a competitive configuration of transfer costs, over the 1960s, as Sylvain Wickham points out, the Rhine axis reached the limits of its potential, and thereafter experienced the restrictive disadvantages of a uni-directional valley geared to traditional manufacturers.* It lacked the flexibility of the coastal plain and the spatial advantages of the extensive basin.

Over the past twenty years the functional shape of Western European economy has thus changed from one dominated by a concentration of energy supply and steel production at the centre, to one in which industry is increasingly regionalised with an emphasis on maritime location and in which the most dynamic and productive areas are to be found in the south. Above all, Europe has become a continental economy whose energy supply is mainly imported.

The growing reliance on oil, that is, has actually reversed the conditions of integration as they existed two decades ago. Italy was only marginally concerned with the origins of the Coal and Steel Community, because she produced little of either commodity. Today she is the fourth largest refiner of oil in the world, while France relies on oil for almost 70 per cent of her total energy supply.

**The new regional division of Europe**

The traditional distinction between the developed centre of Western Europe's economy and the less developed periphery is no longer of any analytical value. The movement from the land has passed the stage where it is merely a reflection

*Sylvain Wickham, *L'Espace Industriel Européen*, Calmann-Levy (Paris, 1969), p. 150.

# SNOWFLAKE DIAGRAMS FOR SELECTED REGIONS
# UNITED KINGDOM   1972

SOURCE: ABSTRACT OF REGIONAL STATISTICS No. 7

C.S.O. LONDON 1972

CHART XXV

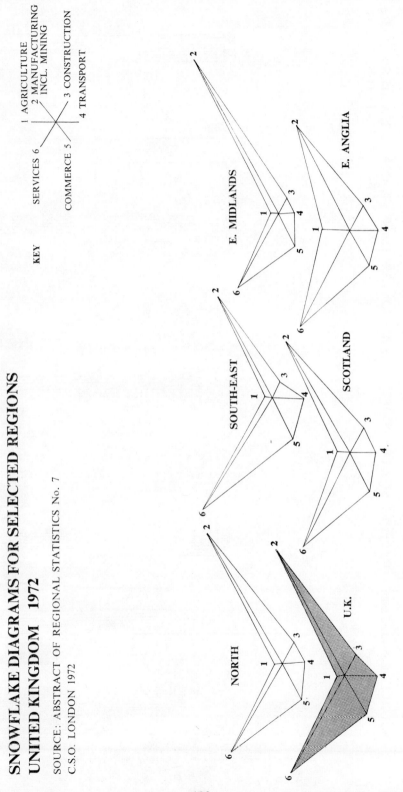

KEY

1 AGRICULTURE
2 MANUFACTURING INCL. MINING
3 CONSTRUCTION
4 TRANSPORT
COMMERCE 5
SERVICES 6

E. MIDLANDS

E. ANGLIA

SOUTH-EAST

SCOTLAND

NORTH

U.K.

# THE GROWTH IN PER CAPITA INCOME IN BRITAIN'S REGIONS 1960-1980

SOURCE: Computed from    RAPPORT SUR LES PROBLEMES REGIONAUX DANS LA COMMUNAUTE ELARGIE
(EEC, BRUSSELS (1973) p. 111)

CHART XXVI

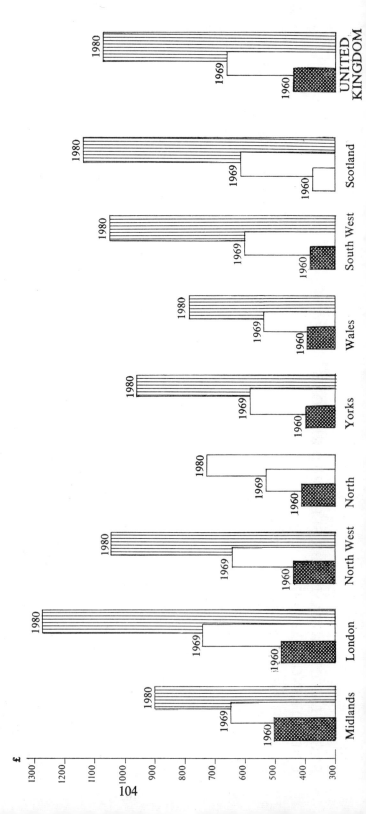

of comparative underdevelopment; indeed, that movement is now becoming obscured by a marked drift back to rural areas in some countries, and certainly in Britain itself. More important, many of the poor European regions of the 1950s are the buoyant or growing regions of the 1970s. Unfortunately, this is not to say that public policy has recognised these changes: at the EEC level there has been little adjustment to these developments. Brussels regional policy still reflects the traditional philosophy of coal and steel, a notion which is about two decades out of date.* And in many national capitals within the Nine regional planning continues to be based on the orthodoxy of European economic relations. In West Germany, for example, there remain considerable constitutional and regional political barriers to any ambitious regional programme. This has meant that while two West German Länder (or administrative regions), North Rhine Westphalia and Baden-Württemberg, between them account for an overwhelming 45 per cent of West Germany's total gross domestic product, and over half the country's exports, it has proved practically impossible to adopt central policies on regional change that might eventually correct this threatening imbalance in the national economy, an imbalance that has serious long-term implications for income variations, investment levels and central economic management. An important reason for this difficulty in arriving at a workable regional policy has been, of course, the strong decentralising spirit of the Federal Republic constitution of 1949, which gives considerable fiscal and economic management powers to the regions themselves, sometimes to the detriment of central government efforts at overall structural reform. Additionally, there have always been fears that changing regional boundaries or re-defining the relationship between the administrative Länder and the central powers in Bonn could affect the prospects for any re-unification of the Federal Republic with the territories that are now East Germany. The inability of West German governments to act more energetically to restructure the regional balance is one important factor in the problematic future that the West German economy faces in the mid-1970s.

Elsewhere, more developed regional planning mechanisms exist. In France such planning has become a central factor in the comparative resilience of the economy overall. French regional planning does, it is true, have a very long history—there was a flourishing movement in academic and administrative circles even in the late nineteenth century—but it became effective only when organised within the context of planned national economic growth. Such planned growth has succeeded in generating an impressive stability in economic performance over twenty years, and at base largely explains the rapid expansion of the French economy in the post-war period.†

But the Plans around which governmental policy revolved only became fully successful when their orientation expressed a dynamic notion of the economy's

*For discussion of this see James Bellini, "Europe of Regions in the 1980s", *Futures*, London, June 1974.
†Hudson Europe, *L'Envol de la France*, Hachette (Paris 1973).

future shape. The First Plan, for example, which ran from 1947 to 1953, concentrated only on sectoral assistance designed to return major basic industries such as coal, steel, electricity and transport, to viability through channelling heavy investment funds into them. There was no real attempt to define the spatial requirements of France's postwar economy, of how it might be restructured, and in which areas it might now develop. Criticism of the First Plan's objectives was widespread, not least because by favouring the traditional regions in the North, in Lorraine and around Paris, the First Plan actually accentuated existing regional differences.* Significantly, France's impressive rate of growth did not become established until the operation of the Second Plan after 1954, with its greater emphasis on dispersing production to all parts of the country.

At the head of this changed regional policy represented in the Second Plan was a greater commitment to structural mobility within the economy: of shifting new kinds of production to new regions, of creating regional infrastructure as foundations for local growth, and of giving greater influence in regional expansion schemes to the contribution of the major provincial cities. But mobility, and the planning themes that went with it, required a redefinition of the geographic form of the economy as it would increasingly become in years ahead. Thus, an integral part of the regional planning process, in alliance with the National Economic Plans, was the elaboration of plans for the future. As a result of consistent policies on regional issues the French record on reducing regional inequalities of income and productive infrastructure has been quite good. The age-old predominance of Paris has been reduced and regions long regarded as rural backwaters have been brought closer to economic conditions obtaining in the developed zones. It is probable that regional discrepancies will be progressively eliminated in the 1980s, given the continuation of French regional policy. There seems an obvious lesson in this for a Britain whose impoverished regions have been left largely unaffected by all of the regional aid provided in recent decades.

---

*Hugh D. Clout, *The Geography of Post-War France*, Pergamon Press (Oxford 1972) p. 23.

CHART XXVII

# EUROPEAN REGIONAL PER CAPITA INCOME: 1985

European Average: $6257 ($ at 1969 rate).

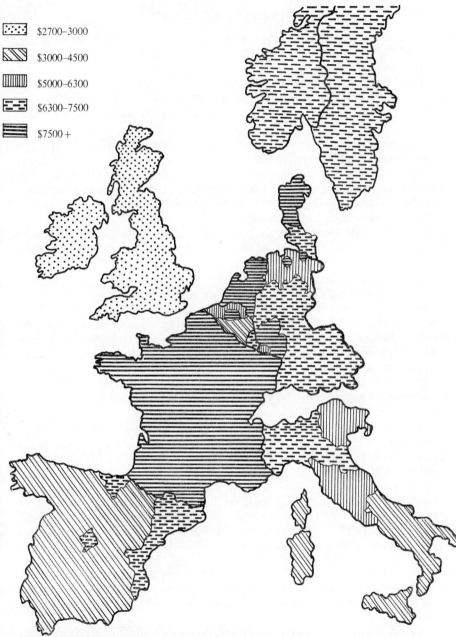

$2700–3000

$3000–4500

$5000–6300

$6300–7500

$7500+

DATA FROM OSCE REGIONAL STATISTICS EEC. 1972.
THOMSON REPORT. 1973
OECD NATIONAL ACCOUNTS. 1953–1969.
1985 PROJECTION BASED ON 1960's ANNUAL AVERAGE REGIONAL GROWTH RATES AT
CURRENT PRICES.
REPRINTED FROM ARTICLE BY JAMES BELLINI. EUROPE OF REGIONS IN THE 1980's
*FUTURES*, VOL. 6, NO. 3, JUNE 1974.

# CHAPTER VI

## WHAT IS TO BE DONE

Meanwhile England, together with the rest of the world, is changing. And like everything else it can change only in certain directions, which up to a point can be foreseen. That is not to say that the future is fixed, merely that certain alternatives are possible and others not. A seed may grow or not grow, but at any rate a turnip seed never grows into a parsnip.

> George Orwell: *England Your England*

Considering the future has never been a popular British pastime. In part this aversion stems from the regard the country has for its past, a regard that has manifested itself in a body of historical scholarship of unrivalled standard. It has been further nourished by the fact that England's expansion and later ascendancy from, say, the sixteenth century, stands in stark historical contrast to the less encouraging realities of today. The reading public seems to have taken refuge in the contemplation of ages that are now past. British television is replete with sagas and serials on the themes of kingship or imperial virtues.

But there is also a strong resistance to the very notion of studying the probable course of future developments—a resistance that cannot simply be explained by this same taste for historical narrative, or indeed by any general suspicion that the future can only be bleak and foreboding. In France, for example, deeply imbedded in their culture exists an even more entrenched traditional sense of Jansenism, of pessimism about future developments. Voltaire's *Candide*, arguably one of the greatest of French literary essays is, after all, based almost entirely on the theme of optimism versus questioning and doubt, and remains a monument to scepticism about the long-term outcome for mankind.

Yet this characteristic of French society did not prevent it, at the same time, from establishing, at a very early point, a tradition of serious thought about the future. Turgot had helped establish that tradition as early as 1750; Sébastien Mercier published his book of prophecy, *The Year 2440*, in 1770. He looked to a world free of slavery, with popular education and socially-just political systems.* And since then that tradition has slowly evolved into a habit of planning and assessment of future national objectives that now runs through the entire system of France's economic management—in industry, in regional policy, in social infrastructure.

In Britain that evolution into planning the future has not taken place. Attempts to make serious assessments of future developments in Britain's society and economy, as we ourselves have discovered, have been greeted, certainly in

---

*He also looked to a permanent end to war between France and England, a prediction that may yet come true.

many academic and administrative quarters, with reactions ranging from dismissive scepticism to utter hostility. In some respects, it is true, such reactions are the product of serious disillusionment with the contributions of quantitative analysis over the years to solving the mounting economic problems the country has faced. Certainly in the field of the social sciences (if indeed the social sciences can ever be regarded as such, so tenuous have their claims to be exact or predictive become), this disdain has been strongly reinforced. Despite the fact that early efforts in political economy were not without strong tendencies to predict and thereby to prescribe—the work of the Reverend T. R. Malthus in population growth being a prime example—none of the social sciences has come any closer, in over a century and a half, to a predictive theory of any worth. Even Malthus himself, having staked a claim to immortality with studies suggesting impending world over-population, was finally obliged to concede the repeated failures to assess, with any scientific accuracy, the future development of entities in which impetuous humanity played a part. As he was to put it in later life: "We should fall into a serious error if we were to suppose that any propositions, the practical results of which depend upon the agency of so variable a being as man and the qualities of so variable a compound as the soil, can ever admit of the same kinds of proof, or lead to the same conclusions, as those which relate to figure and number".*

The failure in Britain to see futures research as in some respects a practical extension of history, geography, sociology and politics has robbed the country of the ability to develop notions about its own future that could serve as a practical basis for discussion and, perhaps, policy.

Peter Laslett, in concluding *The World We Have Lost*, an admirable study of the social fabric of 17th century England, felt compelled to make clear his own conclusions about the purpose of historical analysis. It had the function, he said, of helping a society "understand itself in time"; more important, perhaps, it gave one the capacity to "understand by contrast", to place the present in a dynamic context. And in that process the work of the historian was important, but not overriding; nor was the exact statistical precision of the economist, now all-hallowed in an age of statistics, of unalloyed value. Complex questions of social change required breadth of intellectual experience and a catholicity of techniques that could only ideally come from the co-operative work of several intellectual disciplines.†

The theme can be carried further. Assessing the course of the next fifteen years is very much a question of ranging alternatives against the present, of creating a view of the decade or so ahead that stands in contrast to the facts of today. In

---

*Rev. T. R. Malthus, *Principles of Political Economy Considered with a View to Their Practical Application* (London 1820), pp. 1-2.

†Peter Laslett, *The World We Have Lost* (London 1971) p. 244. He continues: "Too great a reliance in the past on exclusively economic analysis has led to all the sterilities of the economic interpretation of history."

some respects, clearly, the broad outlines within which those alternatives are to be sketched are already determined; after all, as we have noted above, the investments or public policy decisions of today become fully effective only five or ten years hence. For example, the programme for the research and development of Concorde was agreed to as far back as 1962, while any major development project approved today by, say, the National Coal Board could not be fully operational this side of 1980. But there is also a need to create an image of the attainable future which enshrines tested values and yet provides semi-permanent axes of change, an image which allows for continuity of expectations and an element of self-fulfilment. Yet before even such an image can be evolved there has to be a generalised commitment to the future itself. It is this preliminary commitment that Britain lacks.

The absence of any strong commitment to future change has meant the misuse or even destruction of key elements of Britain's social, intellectual and economic reserves that would under different conditions represent considerable assets. Many of these elements—like the stability of its political system, the innate sense of fairness in public debate and the capacity to compromise—are still the well-polished currency of foreign opinion about Britain. But they are falling under increasing strain as the tensions that economic pressures generate invade the processes of negotiation or setting of priorities that make up the daily round in government and manufacturing. At a less abstract level, the qualities of intellectual strength, of technological competence, and of the economic resilience that traditionally derived from Britain's status as an island—and an island of considerable regional variations—have not been fully exploited. To some degree this resulted from the barriers to change that class or convention erected. These barriers were also the damaging consequences of an inadequate perception of the very direction of change. The two acting together, social inertia and the absence of objectives, could not help but produce a general condition of stagnation and drift.

### The Victorian legacy

Britain in the 1970s is very largely the creation of the mid-Victorian period. This fact, while it carries with it some of the positive legacies of Victorian Britain into the contemporary world, also accounts for the greater part of contemporary Britain's weaknesses. Many of the country's problems are Victorian problems, or stem from attempts to operate Victorian solutions in a society that exists in a late twentieth-century world. In a nutshell, Victorian Britain attempted to come to terms with a crude industrialism; the Britain of the 1970s has refused to look beyond it.

Coming to terms with the social and economic realities of Victorian Britain meant asking questions about the society of that time that are strikingly similar to those raised today. But the solutions that today must be sought cannot borrow from the outmoded norms of the 1880s any more than lessons learnt in the administration of British India can apply to issues of, say, Britain's

110

regional devolution in the 1970s. That modern Britain has not moved further than posing those same questions in over a hundred years is moreover a pertinent comment on the stagnation of modern Britain's pace of political change.

In short, the Britain of the 1860s and 1870s was required to ask itself what kind of industrial society it was to have, and how the tensions that such a society would increasingly generate were to be mitigated. It is true that the electoral reforms of 1832 had amended the rules of the political game in favour of certain new classes, and that the Britain of the mid-century held an unrivalled position as a manufacturer and trader (between 1840 and 1870 world trade grew by some 500 per cent, with Britain a major beneficiary) but it was yet to come to terms, for instance, with the urban desolation and complex problems of social re-organisation that rampant industrialism had brought. It was yet to define its own circumstances. In the event, Victorian Britain defined its new situation by making a compromise between the existing form of social structure and its economic and intellectual potential. The society still lives with that compromise.

The years around 1870 were punctuated with legislative and social innovation, changes that stemmed in part from a resolve to set, from a position of clear economic leadership, a model for the civilised world. The Britain of 1870 was, after all, the most prosperous son of the Industrial Revolution, and perhaps even felt that it could afford the luxury of altering the social foundations of a traditional structure. The 1867 Reform Act extended the franchise well beyond the limited scope of the 1832 legislation; further broadening came in 1874 and 1884. The higher posts in the civil service were opened to competitive examination for the first time. In 1873 the bewildering mass of convention and legal form that passed for English law was refined and partially codified in a Judicature Act which brought a limited uniformity to an important social mechanism. The Education Act which brought a national system of elementary education came in 1870. A local government board was established. In 1871 a Trade Union Act and a consolidating Factory and Workshops Act appeared. Laws on liquor licensing, the political status of the armed forces and the functioning of the limited liability company were added to a lengthening list of regulatory or innovative instruments without precedent in English parliamentary history.*

There was, however, a crucial flaw in this process of adaptation. For, underlying these decisions to modify the operational characteristics of British society was a generalised belief among members of the political and administrative élite that Britain would continue to be the dominant industrial force in the developed world, a belief that was already, by the 1870s, demonstrably unrealistic. The result was a synthesising of elements of reform with a failing economic vitality, a series of social enactments introduced into a situation of economic decline.

---

*For a full discussion see Michael Fores, *Britain's Economic Growth and the 1870 Watershed*, Lloyds Bank Review (London), 1 January 1971.

The issues posed in the Britain of a century ago were not, as some contemporary reformers thought, ones of subtle or partial modification of social and political structure—extension of the franchise here, rationalisation of trade union status there. They were issues that arose because of the incipient weaknesses characteristic of British society in an industrial age—weaknesses that were truly to threaten Britain with the permanent position of being "workshop of the world" —a place of manual tasks and depressing factory life. The issues at stake were those of re-orientating British society to fit it for the high industrialism of the twentieth century, and these issues were evaded.

For the Britain of Victoria's day was not at the zenith of its power: it was already well beyond it. Although the introduction of those popular items that have been regarded as the certain sign of a mass-consumption society—the bicycle, the safety match, the advertising hoarding—suggested an economy in full flood, serious questions were being asked in more contemplative quarters about the long-term prospects. A Royal Commission on the Depression in Trade and Industry, reported in the mid-1880s that the economy was beginning "to feel the effect of foreign competition in quarters where our trade formerly enjoyed a practical monopoly". While British exports of coal mounted dramatically, and were regarded by those in high places as vindication of their faith in the economy's overwhelming strength, it needed only a slight degree of cynicism to conclude also that those very exports pointed to the rapid industrialisation of rivals abroad. British investment in her industries lagged behind levels in the United States and Germany and invention after invention slipped out of the hands of British manufacturers to be exploited and refined elsewhere.* The Britain of 1870, in fact, was a mirror-image of the Britain of today; as David Landes put it in the *Cambridge Economic History of Europe:* "[in 1870] all the evidence agrees on the technological backwardness of much of British manufacturing industry—on leads lost, opportunities missed, markets relinquished that might not have been."

The foundations of present-day Britain were therefore laid on the shifting soil of a failing economy, and were so designed that the social disjunctions that were component parts of that inherent weakness were actually buttressed in the name of reform. And there were two important reasons why this was so. First, there was little real incentive for change in an establishment then still believing— erroneously—that it commanded an unassailable economic bastion. The establishment was not prepared to alter the society that guaranteed its own position, especially when it was convinced that the society's strength in fact rested on an organisation and cohesion it had itself fostered over generations. Second, there was no comprehensive view held in political circles of that time about the nature of Britain's future beyond vague insistence that tomorrow could only be a more glorious and more prosperous extension of the Imperial present, an insistence that was built into the social fabric itself. As a result the potential strengths

---

*H. Pelling, *Modern Britain 1885-1955* (London 1969), ch. 2.

available to the society in the economic sphere were dissipated. What might have been assets were progressively rendered inconsequential or simply wasted through mismanagement. In essence, then, we suggest that Britain once and for all break with its Victorian past, and renew in these closing years of the late twentieth century the process of social and psychological evolution that has been in abeyance for nearly a century.

**The needs of the present day**

That we say "in abeyance for nearly a century" may astonish some. Were there not important political reforms on the eve of the First World War? Important social legislation under the aegis of Labour after the Second? But we have spoken of "social and psychological" evolution—and we would say that the fundamental "feel" of British society has hardly altered in a century. Only the economic decline has gone on, with its characteristic embittering of quasi-Victorian social relationships.

What we call for, then, is both simple and immense—a shift in Britain's national style. Faced with the intellectual and moral dilemmas we have examined (for the dilemmas before Britain are not merely economic ones) the question of what Britain should *do* cannot really be answered with any list of new programmes or of innovations in technique. The popular and professional literature on Britain's plight suffers from no shortage of practical suggestions. Clearly, a hundred reports of investigatory commissions have recommended most of the specific suggestions we shall make in the following pages. What is to be done is not all that difficult to say—nor is there any question that to the problem of Britain's failing economy a whole series of attractive answers exist, depending on whether one prescribes for Britain from the standpoint of right or left or centre.

Certainly no specific remedies will work for Britain if there is not a shift, a deep shift, in psychology, in will—in short, in style. For style in this case is everything. Everything that follows then must be understood as subordinate to this. For style is the habit of action and decision that derives from those assumptions about political and economic reality. We would argue that Britain's present economic difficulties and social difficulties derive ultimately from a kind of archaism of the society and national psychology: a habit of conciliation in social and personal relations for its own sake, a lack of aggression, a deference to what exists, a repeated and characteristic flight into pre-industrial, indeed pre-capitalist, fantasies, a suspicion of efficiency as somehow "common", a dislike for labour itself—all of course accompanied by a deep inner rage at the frustrations and obfuscations which contemporary Britain demands of its citizens and an equally significant envy for the wordly goods that others, Americans, Belgians, Germans, French, have and which the stodgy pattern of a more traditionalist British society and economy cannot provide.

113

What follows is only a partial list, and in some cases a list of the obvious. We repeat, in themselves they are not sufficient. But accompanied by a new will to succeed, these, and other remedies, would begin to cure the malignant "British disease". Whether these, or similar proposals will be adopted, is an open question. For as a despairing *arbitrista*, one of those seventeenth-century Spanish economists who wrote incessantly of their nation's accelerating decline, sadly put it: "Alas, I do not think much will be done. For those who can will not—and those who will cannot."*

We are struck repeatedly by the parallels between Britain and 17th century Spain. As J. H. Eliott puts it: "But, behind this inert government, which possessed neither the courage nor the will to look its weakness squarely in the face lay a whole social system and a psychological attitude which themselves blocked the way to radical reform. That injection of new life into the Castillian economy . . . would have required a vigorous display of personal enterprise, a willingness and ability to invest in agrarian and industrial projects . . . and to make use of the most recent technical advances. None of them was forthcoming."† We feel they are parallels to be avoided.

**A national development plan**

We have made it explicit throughout this study that the critical condition of British industry, and of the economy for which it is the base, results from a long history of low investment, vaguely-defined or non-existent longer-term objectives, and a failure to carry innovation into the practical realm of production and marketing. Britain has invested too little at home, often in the wrong industries and on the basis of chance rather than for concrete and practical goals. Investment policy has been handicapped by the perennial shortage of domestic funds that the City's predilection for exporting capital has guaranteed, while the structural framework for ongoing investment strategy has remained the object of political disagreement for decades.

It seems self-evident to us that a major re-orientation of the British economy can result only from comprehensive provisions for industrial and infrastructure investment on a national scale and within the context of a continuous medium-term planning process. To the outside observer such a recommendation appears so glaringly essential that, indeed, it is difficult to elaborate new reasoning that might at last bring to fruitful conclusion a very old debate. Nevertheless, we intend setting out, for the record, the proposals that inexorably emerge from the facts and analyses on the preceding pages.

Our principal recommendation is that economic policy should become the province of a new national six-year plan under the aegis of the state. This is, in effect, to ask that Britain join the ranks of modern, technocratic, growth-

---

*Carlo Cipolla, ed. *The Economic Decline of Empires* (New York, 1972), p. 153.
†See J. H. Eliott, in Carlo Cipolla, ed., op. cit., p. 153.

orientated societies—not so much those of the Eastern bloc as to follow the lead, however unpalatable or wounding to Britain's national pride, of a country like France. We have stressed elsewhere, and do not wish to repeat a well-worn theme, that it is the French economy, not the *laissez-faire* economy of West Germany, which has registered the most satisfactory sustained growth performance in the postwar era. While it cannot be denied that France's problems since 1945 have been far less daunting than Britain's, for one thing, France's economic growth has resulted from that nation's not truly ever having had an industrial revolution prior to the close of World War II, while Britain's problems are those of an aged industrial economy, it would seem to us that the need for a similar planning process is virtually self-evident.

We suggest, be it noted, a six year plan—in the deliberate attempt to make clear that this plan must not be allowed to become a political football. The maximum life of any parliament being five years, we would stress an apolitical, or better still, suprapolitical nature for this plan. The intention is to articulate national goals over the long term—to assure to industry and the regions of Britain a security of investment environment which alone can permit regeneration.

We suggest, also, that the plan become the province of Britain's best economists and administrators and engineers, all serving the nation in a self-conscious spirit of ambition (for the country) and enterprise. Those working for the plan, for the national investment and development corporation (see over), and the dynamic industries associated with them, should come in time to see themselves as a new élite—not an arrogant technocratic bureaucracy beyond political control, but one committed to the restructuring of Britain and to its regeneration. There is not, in our opinion, any real contradiction between democracy and such a long-term planning group. Planning mechanisms on the continent do not necessarily escape from ultimate parliamentary control; indeed a select or standing parliamentary committee, bi-partisan, or multi-partisan, should work with the planners to ensure a responsiveness to the basic will of the country and a continuity of policy as governments change. We are thus *not* recommending a benign totalitarianism for Britain; nor even rule by technocrats. We are recommending the intelligent modern use of technocrats in the service of the democratic state.

We understand that to develop such a responsible élite, ambitious for their country, divorced from petty politics and the narrow economic ideologies of the various parties, will not be easy. But it was not easy in the nineteenth century to develop a paid, professional, and impartial civil service, yet Britain did so and led the world. Other nations like Italy, apart from the state banking authorities and the state industrial managers (of IRI, ENI, etc.) have not been able to produce a disinterested and reliable civil service even yet. What we are asking, then, is that in a new spirit of practicality the best brains of Britain be put to the task of analysing the society's economic needs, articulating regional plans, industrial

115

plans, and long-range goals for the country as a whole, in contrast to the drift, evasion, and sentimentality that has characterised economics in Britain at least since 1945.

In this respect, we ask for a commission of the plan to be divided into three directorates—the national planning directorate, the regional planning director- ate, and a directorate for science and advanced technology.

The directorate for regional planning needs a word of explanation. We believe that it is insufficiently understood in Britain how overcentralised the nation has become. It is a commonplace of political wisdom that France is an over- centralised nation—though efforts there are now being made to reverse this situation. Britain, however, is nearly as centralised as France, and with the palpable, and unfavourable difference, that its centralising Whitehall bureau- cracy has tended to be undynamic and unambitious for the country. In Britain, then, there should be a devolution of considerable powers to the regions, of which the power to plan, within the larger and co-ordinated national context, is only one part of the picture. For the regions of Britain (be they the historic counties and kingdoms, or some new affinity grouping on the basis of geography and economic standing) might also begin to approach the powers of the American states—granted the right to levy an expanded range of taxes, including income taxes at modest levels, in order to attract and sustain desirable economic activities.

It is our belief that such regional plans, brought to the central planning authority through the regional planning directorate, could powerfully stimulate the local economies—not merely to maintain employment through labour-intensive industry, but to seek out technology-intensive activities which alone can sustain a country like Britain in the years ahead. For while we accept the necessity to maintain full employment in Britain, the country must phase out labour- intensive, low-technology industries as rapidly as decently can be done. Britain, in a time when countries like Iran, South Korea, and Brazil have already begun to manufacture automobiles, ships, cheap textiles, and basic consumer electrical goods, cannot pay its way with industries like these.

Britain must become a centre for technology and capital-intensive industries, a generator of new processes and new devices, a home of knowledge-related economic activities—in keeping with a traditional genius.

### A National Investment and Development Corporation

Our next proposal is that investment in valuable but troubled industries (as a means of salvage), and in advanced industries which meet difficulty raising capital (as a means of ensuring that Britain recapture the technological heights), should become the province of a new body of interlocking units under the supervision of the state—an industrial investment corporation. Unfortunately, such a proposal risks falling into the seemingly bottomless pit of suggestions on

116

the subject that some fifty years of trial and error have produced. It runs the risk, too, of becoming yet another addition to a long list of major public owner-ship measures that, ironically, began with the Conservative administration of 1925, with its Electricity Supply Act. And in the context of a newly elected Labour government, with its political programme for extending the public sector, it risks becoming banal.

However, we feel it essential both to distinguish our suggested structure from those efforts that have gone before, whether it be the Industrial Re-organisation Corporation or the currently proposed National Enterprise Board, and somehow to guarantee that it survives. We wish also to distinguish our proposal from nationalistion as such. Our concern in this study is solely with the economic regeneration of Britain—its efficiency—and not with politics or economic philosophy. There is a long-standing debate in Britain on the necessity or folly of nationalisation—but it seems to us that the arguments, for and against, do not properly lie in the area of cost-efficiency analysis. They are, as we have said, political, or even moral, at bottom. We note too that within the ranks of the developed nations there are countries (like France) with a high degree of nationalisation whose economic performance has been highly favourable; and others (like West Germany) with a weakly developed state sector whose econo-mic performance has also been immensely superior to Britain's.

The question is, apart from nationalising the "commanding heights" of the economy, is there another formula for state intervention which is better able to achieve the goal of accelerated economic growth and the stimulation of advanced industry? It seems to us that there is—following the formula of a NIDEC, itself based on the Italian formula of the Institute per la Reconstruzione Industriale (IRI).* In our view Britain's NIDEC should invest in whole, in partnership, and indeed often in minority partnership, in industries which, as we have stated above, are in need of support (while valuable to Britain's economy as a whole) or in need of superior creditworthiness to obtain funds for accelerated research and development, forward planning, or capital (re)equipment.

A National Investment and Development Corporation should then, in our view, be more ambitious than the variety of proposed or actual institutions that have emerged with regularity over the last ten years. The old Industrial Reorganisation Corporation, erected during the Labour administration of 1966-1970, while being a step in the right direction, was both too timid and lacked the means for long-term operational competence. Its very name suggested "reorganisation" of industry and economy rather than the creation of new avenues for change. In addition, though its functions, as defined under the IRC Act, were related to

---

*It should be noted that Italy's present (1974-75) economic difficulties in no way invalidate the mechanism of IRI. It is not the Italian industrial sector that is in trouble or has failed Italy. Indeed, it may well be the most dynamic industrial sector of postwar Europe. It is the Italian government—the traditional party structure and traditional bureaucracy—that have not kept pace, and thereby skewed the economy.

the "promotion, reorganisation or development of any industry", and therefore allowed for considerable initiative in the industrial field, much of the Corporation's early work was too closely identified with traditional manufacturing or those sectors of the economy that should properly be phased out (motor vehicle production, most textiles). Furthermore there was an overlap with planning powers already existing elsewhere—as in the steel industry, which, following nationalisation in 1967, was setting up its own long-term goals. On balance, while the IRC did develop a close interest in some key high and medium technology industries, such as electronics, nuclear power and scientific instruments, these never developed a sense of co-ordinated and long-term purpose that might have provided a basic framework for comprehensive structural change and a greater degree of applied innovation.*

This was a signal weakness, for at the root of much of Britain's economic difficulty, as we have repeatedly stressed, is a failure to carry technological innovation to the factory floor in the shape of improved plant or more advanced productive processes. This is a failure that has influenced the shaping of education policy as well as the structural transformation of industry, and its ramifications have become evident in poor productivity, lack of reliability of products and a growing unsuitability of British manufactured goods for the competitive markets of the developed world.†

The eventual economic consequences of such technical retardation could be immensely damaging. Certainly the depressing record of British industry over the last three decades is primarily due to the inability to make full use of the country's considerable technological reserves. But more particularly, we are convinced that the longer-term cumulative consequences of such lack of technology application would actually be as Jacques Ellul has described it: "If a Byzantine phase of technical arrest were to occur in the economic realm, it would represent not only an arrest of economic evolution but a regression as well, with a resultant series of deep crises."‡

The need for such an institution is pressing—eleven years after that Labour Party Conference in Scarborough at which an era of "white hot technological revolution was ushered in through speeches of the party leadership. The record in this crucial field has remained one of haphazard and disunified policies implemented in a climate of confusion. As one specialist observed recently: "Innovation is fun and also important, but most technology is unspectacular by comparison . . . Unhappily, the past ten years have shown that British governments divide their efforts between rescuing lame ducks and chasing after new industries."§

---

*Industrial Reorganisation Corporation,* Report and Accounts for 1967/8, 1968/9, 1969/70.
†The failures of British manufacturers to innovate are graphically set out in Messrs Nasbeth and Ray, *The Diffusion of New Industrial Processes,* NIESR (London 1974).
‡Jacques Ellul, *The Technological Society,* Random House (New York 1964), p. 151.
§John Maddox, "How the 'white heat' of technology went cold", *The Times,* 3 October, 1973.

In any event the IRC was never to have the opportunity of succeeding as it was abolished by the Conservative government elected in 1970. The new theme of Labour's National Enterprise Board does not, in our view, even consolidate the organisational principles conceded at the time of the creation of IRC. This Board, while admittedly borrowing much from the Italian IRI, which has made a vital contribution to the structural adaptation of the modern Italian economy, also draws at least as heavily on the traditions of Labour Party evangelism on the subject of public ownership. The debate on NEB, that is, has retained much of the punitive sentiment that has characterised the evolution of Labour's policy on industrial reorganisation. The proposal has become inexorably linked to doctrinaire positions on nationalisation, and thereby been made an object of political confrontation. This seems to us to guarantee its fate— to be jettisoned in time, as parliamentary balance or political expediency dictate.

In other respects NEB appears to lack the conceptual strength of IRI, for without the over-arching scheme of national and regional planning machinery geared to producing a high degree of continuity in public policy, any such board cannot easily escape the dilemma of having to function with no guarantee of stable long-term objectives. As a result, projects would be frustrated and personnel disillusioned as initial enthusiasm gave way to repeated conflicts of interest that, for example, came to plague future planning in the British Steel Corporation from 1972.* And while NEB bears the mark of a long-standing hostility to the private sector of industry, so pronounced among the "new" Labour Left, it will find it increasingly difficult to see its role as one of constructive intervention through selective investment or acquisition. For unless such an institution sees its function as that of magnifying progressive trends in the economy as a whole, and eliminating those sectors whose longer-term viability is doubtful, of encouraging "leading edge" processes to the exclusion of labour intensity, then it becomes little more than a cushion against stagnation and economic decline, and a substitute for corrective policy.

Outside the purely political sphere, schemes for massive national investment have abounded. Perhaps the most ambitious was that outlined in a major leading article of *The Times* of 19 December 1973, calling for some £20,000 million to be devoted to re-equipping British industry. In general, the argument was not to be quarrelled with, yet the proposal failed in exactly those areas that were most crucial for any such initiative's eventual success. The funds were to be channelled into industry through the diffuse mechanisms of government-industry collaboration, without any recourse to a more integrated and planned structure, with the risk that the money would be spent without any real co-ordination or close analysis of objectives. More significant, the specific industrial

---

*As one author put it recently: "it is an occupational hazard of being a Chairman of a large nationalised industry to fall prey to the illusion that a paper agreement with the ruling Government Department can 'settle' for ten years ahead things such as the level of steel demand, level of prices, response of the labour force etc." *Crisis in Steel*, Fabian Society, June 1974.

activities that were to benefit from this immense investment programme were exactly those with the least viable long-term outlook—those which in our opinion should be cut back or eventually eliminated. To borrow the wording from *The Times* itself: "One can see the industries in which investment can be made with considerable confidence. There will in 1980 be continuing world demand, including British demand, for cheap steel . . . for cheap small cars . . . for energy from oil . . . for ships . . . for cheap textiles. A programme such as this should concentrate on basic production, which can either be exported directly or fabricated and exported." Yet in our view that describes precisely the programme to be avoided, for it would not only prolong the life of industries that in the long term must prove less and less competitive against new producers abroad, but would also devote vast funds to reconstructing British industry in the classic mould. Under the guise of radical change it would perpetuate Britain as an early industrial state.

The NIDEC which we propose should replace the plethora of bodies, committees and groups that have accumulated in the field of structural management since the war. Moreover, it should become an adjunct to the planning system we have outlined above, so as to permit it to be governed by an evolving long-term economic strategy.

### A national administration college

Neither planning machinery nor investment institution will have major long-term impact unless their administrative and technical skills match the complexity of their task. It is therefore essential that the means be found to stimulate a flow of highly competent people into this integrated planning and investment sector. In our view this flow can only come from outside the existing higher education structure, which is too amorphous and too little committed to practical action and the application of theory to adjust adequately to such a need.

There should be created, then, an administrative academy borrowing much from the French Ecole Nationale d'Administration, a post-graduate school established in the immediate post-war years to train technicians and administrators for the operation of French national and regional Plans. It is an élite, institution, in theory apolitical,* and it operates in parallel to the existing advanced education system. The school has moved from its former emphasis on a traditional and rather legalistic civil service training to concentrate on sociology, economics, and management. It has joined itself to the prestige of those French civil service élites which under the old system were brought into ministries and other public bodies from the *grandes écoles*. The ENA graduate is a very highly trained member of an administrative network which is also a like-thinking fraternity, despite its members being scattered throughout the nation and

---

*Among its early graduates are to be found such politically diverse products as the current French President, Valéry Giscard d'Estaing, Prime Minister Chirac, and the leader of the Unified Socialist Party, Michel Rocard.

economy, in different government departments and different geographic regions. Working under national and regional political authorities, the ENA graduates provide a certain uniformity of style, ability and objective throughout the national administration. There is also a capacity to communicate directly with the higher levels of government on behalf of specific departmental or regional problems simply because of the access that an ENA background ensures: the system provides what is, in a sense, a practical "old boys network" geared to getting things done in the economic and administrative spheres.

Again, comparable proposals have been made in Britain at intervals over the past few years. At the time of the Fulton Commission in the 1960s it was widely believed that such an academy would be created. It was not. Instead, a civil service college, of doubtful relevance to any future planning environment, was set up and the opportunity to establish a distinct, post-graduate institution with clearly defined aims was once again lost.

The value of such an academy could, in our opinion, be greater than merely through its training of a new administrative group. It could acquire a psychological dimension, an organisational *élan*, in which students not only found the path to high rank in administration and economic management clearly visible, but also understood themselves to be agents of a crucial transition in Britain's modern experience. Such an academy would come in time to provide a disproportionate share of the senior staff members of the complex of national and regional planning units outlined above, as well as of the dynamic state-financed industries (and very likely of the dynamic private industries as well). Just as important, perhaps, it would increasingly provide a distinguishable mandarinate *with modern skills and a coherent sense of operational purpose* to replace, by degrees, the traditional (and unambitious and, in important respects, pre-modern) British business élite.

It is clear that such a change at the top of the training hierarchy can have a really effective long-term influence only if it capitalises on improvements in the education system as a whole. We have noted that Britain's record on education is that of insufficient weight of numbers at the university level, despite a high comparative priority given to education spending as an aggregate. In part it seems this comes from a traditional tendency to see in the university a repository for the few brightest, a notion which has counterparts in the way privilege is distributed, or opportunity arranged. Education should be available as a right, at all age levels up to the end of the university stage. In this respect, the university expansion programmes in this century have been too modest by far, though we recognise that there are inherent conceptual reasons why this is so. On balance the Robbins Report represented a major opportunity to reorientate the pattern of university education in the direction of greater availability of student places and a more concise statement of medium-term objectives—but little of consequence materialised. The lack of strong consultative links between secondary schools (and their curriculum reform processes) and the universities themselves

121

is in part responsible for the absence of a defined set of educational priorities running throughout the secondary and university phases.

Until there develops a more integrated approach to priorities in education, stretching from the pre-school through to the most advanced levels, it seems to us that there will always be the risk, if not the certainty, that subjects will too often be studied for the wrong reasons, or at the wrong times, or in the wrong place. There will persist a growing disillusionment of many teachers with their role, and the increasing tendency of potential students to shun higher studies on the grounds of an apparent incompatibility between what they are studying and what they see ahead of them in life. So long as the higher education system remains open to very small numbers, with the technical and teacher-training establishments pushed to the fringe, the kind of administrative academy that we are proposing risks yet again becoming available only to a fairly narrow class. Such an academy, functioning within Britain's present university structure could in practice eventually conform to a traditional hierarchy of privilege, and perpetuate the existing systems of access to social position and national influence.

### Control on capital outflows

We wish to make this recommendation in the briefest possible fashion, in order to avoid any possibility of misunderstanding. We are struck by the disastrous effect of the City of London on the British economy. Without discussing the ideology of the City, it is clear that it has preferred for years to profit from its capital and to nourish foreign enterprises rather than feed or renew the sadly depleted infrastructure of the British industrial economy at home. The economy of the UK has thus been subjected to the vicious cycle of "stop-go" to defend the international position of the pound. In the resulting climate of restrictions and uncertainty, investment has always slackened.

It is of course true that investment abroad has traditionally contributed to Britain's inward flow of "invisibles" and helped to keep down Britain's balance of payments deficit, but it is internal industry and commerce which have had to pay the price.\* Moreover, as we have demonstrated in Chapter II in recent years earnings abroad have not equalled the capital outflow. And even if the City could demonstrate that it might in time become "profitable" again, the money would still be more efficiently spent at home whereby a newly efficient British industry could earn much more.

---

\*It is only in one of the five past decades that the resources of the City of London have been directed to the benefit of the internal British economy, and strikingly enough it was in the period of the 1930s that the British economy registered a period of rapid growth. After having suspended the convertibility of the pound in 1931, the government restricted loans abroad, a measure which was eventually softened to permit loans to the Empire. Stimulated by flexible monetary policy, the British economy of the 1930s, even while a world-wide depression raged, paradoxically knew an era of accelerated growth and innovation. The results achieved in this period contrast markedly with those of succeeding years when, once again, the City returned to its customary role—that of the "money pump" of British capital to more enticing regions abroad.

It seems to us clear that Britain cannot any longer afford to allow the City freedom of action on the scale known in postwar years. If it is true that a mature economy (like the West German at the present time, or the United States economy throughout the postwar decades) will tend to send capital abroad for higher returns, still Britain as a superannuated economy, and not merely a mature one, cannot any longer afford the practice. *There can be no renovation of British industry and commerce without a strict limitation on such outflows.* Nor should Britain's multinational corporations be allowed to escape scrutiny on the proportion of earnings abroad repatriated to the benefit of the nation at large.

The City has damaged the British postwar economy in another respect. There has been what might be called an internal "brain drain" toward the City—so that the best minds have gravitated toward the gentlemanly, but frequently unproductive, careers of broker or private banker rather than to the more "common", and often less personally rewarding, positions of industrial management. To restrict the City would be, over the long run, to force these good brains, inefficiently used so far as the British economy as a whole is concerned, toward a dynamic industrial sector.*

### The hereditary peerage

The question of the hereditary peerage in modern Britain no doubt is trivial in its practical effect at the same time that it seems to us weighed with symbolic importance. An essentially agrarian and feudal rank formally occupies the leading position in the social hierarchy of the country and its hierarchy of honour. Individuals who enjoy this status also have a rôle in government which they acquire by inheritance and not by service. If Britain is fully to come to terms with the contemporary world it seems to us of considerable symbolic and psychological importance that this anomaly be ended, and that the House of Lords be reserved to life peers named by reason of their service to the country. It obviously should be made possible for an hereditary peer who gives signal service to be admitted to the House for life; and it may well be that there would be men or women honoured for service who would wish to enter the Upper House without accepting a title. The essential point, in our view, is that the House of Lords become a place for senior counsellors of state who have merited that role by their intellectual and scientific contributions to the society, their services to the country and its economy and industry, or their services to the community.

We are aware of the controversial nature of this proposal—and we are aware as well what the response is likely to be. But we feel, nevertheless, that Britain should bring itself into conformity with the other advanced democracies of North-Western Europe—the Netherlands, Norway, Sweden, Denmark—all of

---

*At present the City of London eschews industry. It is striking how little City money is invested in the exploitation of North Sea oil.

which are monarchies of the best sort, but none of which are societies in which hereditary privilege plays so wide a role.*

Britain needs economic and industrial modernisation, but also a modernisation of a rather different sort. The country needs a fundamental improvement in class relations and social attitudes as they relate to work and trade; and indeed the claims here are of justice as well as efficiency. Britain today maintains its grip on the imagination of Europeans and Americans exactly because, as a society, it seems to them in crucial respects pre-modern.

There is an essentially agricultural and even feudal *style* of Britain as it presents itself to the world; but perhaps also as it presents itself to itself. One knows that the actual material significance on the life of modern Britain of the peerage, of landlords and estates, of the life depicted in *The Field*, is not great. Foreigners understand that the country-house existence, the guards regiments and clubland mystique, the adventures of the titled described in *Country Life*, make up a kind of good-natured fraud in which the foreign readers and visitors themselves are complicitors.

But there is something else that foreigners understand. They take these things as holiday, and they go home to reality. They put down the Michael Innes novel, turn off the television after the Pallisers is concluded, and go on to other things. The British, for all their national scepticism, must live with the myths of gentlemanly amateurism, of aristocratic diffidence towards trade, the social pressures that send successful businessmen to the grouse moors in the autumn to play the role of countryman, and cause the upward-climbing entrepreneur to send his son to Eton and into the City, and make honest trade union leaders covet a peerage and an invitation to luncheon at Boodles. Britain is a nation which in modern times has not had its revolution. That is the real fascination it has to Europeans, Americans and now the Japanese. Britain is an archaeological site from the Western past, full of entrancing and mysterious survivals and archaisms. The European nations and even the United States have been through events that Britain has escaped. They have had social and political revolutions, catastrophic upheavals and class struggles, had societies turned inside out by the forces of democratisation and equalisation and egalitarianism and vulgarisation. They understand what these things have cost and continue to cost; but this also gives them a quality of a modern maturity which we suspect does not really exist in Britain—although it is coming. Britain today is under these kinds of pressures; a kind of quiet revolution is struggling to happen. But the revolution has not yet happened, and it may not come off; and until it does Britain is separated from Europe by an archaism of society that attracts but also rather disquiets the foreigner.

It is dangerous to attempt to analyse the assumptions of another society, yet

---

*It is our belief that this proposal would have the effect of *strengthening* the monarchy, rather than the reverse.

124

there is a strange fact which must be recorded. Arthur Koestler put it very well in an address to the British academy in 1973. He remarked on how extra-ordinary outsiders find the refusal of the British even to admit the reality, the existence, of what he called the "strongly and resentfully held" class divisions of the country, divisions which he regarded as leading to "psychological malaise and economic misadventure". This is exactly our experience. In presenting our preliminary thoughts on the problems of Britain to British audiences over the last year and a half we have found that any introduction of the class issue, any attempt to make dispassionate comment on the nature of class attitudes in the country produces, either passionate denials of the very existence of class barriers or the assertion that they differ in no way from the class structures of any other country. Admittedly our audiences were mainly of middle and professional classes with a presumed stake in denial; but to us—Dutch, French, Americans—this has seemed a very bizarre reaction. We have also found that any attempt to persist on the subject evoked so passionate and emotion-laden an exchange and so resolute a series of diversions of the argument and displace-ments of discussion onto less threatening subjects, that everything else we had to say was lost. Thus we have concluded that to talk about class in this book risks damaging the effect of whatever else we may be able to contribute to the British debate. But we have also concluded that the class issue, which evokes so profound and repressed a series of anxieties, is, as in a primitive society, the national taboo. To discuss it is a revolutionary act; but the question which remains in our mind is what will happen to Britain as it continues to go on unquestioned, unapproached?

* * *

Britain's assets are formidable but their redeployment to the country's economic recovery is extraordinarily difficult, as the events of recent years have shown. There are technical and administrative problems which inhibit structural change in the economy, but there is also an obstacle much harder to describe in a tan-gible way. A problem lies in the outlook of the nation, the attitude of the nation. Thus calls for reform too often come down to pointless invocations of the "Dunkirk spirit", or else the debate on reform turns into a battle on class lines, with vaguely authoritarian calls for national discipline heard on the one side, and on the other, proposals for drastic change that more often than not reveal a punitive spirit—directed not at improving the economy but at punishing the bosses.

There has to be a big change in national attitude, but no one seems very clear how this is to be brought about short of a national catastrophe bringing down the existing system of assumptions, attitudes, and habits of work and manage-ment. The war caused Britain to change, but what today is to serve for what William James called the "moral equivalent of war"? It is this moral equivalent of war that people are looking for when they invoke Dunkirk, and "The Few"; but the truth is that there is no such thing in the economic and social orders.

In the War everyone understood with utter simplicity and urgency that the country was on the edge of a catastrophe. At the same time everyone understood the practical things that had to be done. War simplifies all. Economic decline merely muddles and confuses all. No one knows really what to do, and no one can feel any conviction that individual action will make the slightest difference. Suppose that the Dunkirk spirit could be revived; what would happen? Exactly what would people be expected to do? Even if they did the obvious things, and managers worked harder, and workers did not strike, and traders cut their margins, and people saved and reduced their buying of imports, would that make any difference to the real problems of the economy?

The needed changes are structural.

# About the Authors:

**Edmund Stillman** is Director of Hudson Institute Europe. Formerly attached to the U.S. Department of State, he was subsequently Professor of International Affairs at the Johns Hopkins School of Advanced International Studies, Washington, D.C. He has written many books, three of them in collaboration with William Pfaff, including *The Politics of Hysteria* and *Power and Impotence*. He directed the study on France's future published in 1973, and a report on the future of Paris commissioned in 1974 by the office of the Paris Prefect. He is a graduate of Yale and holds a J.D. from Columbia. He is a member of the New York Bar.

**James Bellini** is British and a student of international affairs and development issues. He studied at Cambridge and the London School of Economics and subsequently was Lecturer in International Politics at the University of Birmingham. He collaborated on Hudson Europe reports on France and on Paris, writes regularly for European newspapers and journals, and has published for the Fabian Society, most recently the pamphlet *British Entry, Labour's Nemesis*. In November 1974 he published *French Defence Policy*, a study commissioned by the Royal United Services Institute for Defence Studies.

**William Pfaff** is an American writer and commentator on political and economic affairs. He has written many books, some in collaboration with Edmund Stillman. He recently published *Condemned to Freedom: the Crisis of Western Liberalism*. He was co-author of the Hudson Europe studies on France and the future of Paris. He contributes regularly to the New Yorker Magazine.

**Laurence Schloesing** is French and an economist. She is a graduate of the University of Paris and completed a Masters degree at Columbia. Before joining Hudson Europe she was an economic analyst with the First National City Bank. Mlle. Schloesing collaborated on the study on France's future and was rapporteur for the report on the development of Paris.

**Michael Barth** has studied in Holland, Italy and the United States. He holds degrees from Brandeis and the School of Advanced International Studies at Johns Hopkins. He is a native of Amsterdam.